My Favourite Animal Stories

Gerald Durrell, whose love and sympathy for animals is known to thousands through his delightful books, his television appearances and his zoo in Jersey, is specially well qualified to select his favourite animal stories for other people's enjoyment. His choice ranges from Arthur Grimble's true account of an octopus hunt to the story of Mowgli's rescue from the Monkey-People in Kipling's *First Jungle Book*, and there is something to please everyone in this collection of stories which are funny, sad, exciting or just plain entertaining.

My Favourite Animal Stories

Edited by Gerald Durrell

Beaver Books
for
Scholastic Publications

First published in 1962 by
Lutterworth Press
Luke House, Farnham Road, Guildford,
Surrey, England
This paperback edition published in 1976 by
The Hamlyn Publishing Group Limited
London · New York · Sydney · Toronto
Astronaut House, Feltham, Middlesex, England
Reprinted 1976
Special Scholastic edition 1976

© Copyright Introduction Gerald Durrell 1962
© Copyright Illustrations Lutterworth Press 1962
ISBN 0 600 36264 7

Printed in England by
Cox & Wyman Limited
London, Reading and Fakenham

Line drawings by Reg Gray
Cover photographs by Phillip Coffey

Acknowledgements

The publishers are much indebted to the following for permission to include material which is their copyright:

John Murray (Publishers) Ltd., for "Assignment with an Octopus" from *A Pattern of Islands* by Arthur Grimble.

David Higham Associates Ltd., and William Collins Sons & Co. Ltd., for "The Boar Hunt" from *The Sword in the Stone* by T. H. White.

The Bodley Head, and A. M. Heath & Co. Ltd., for "Seal Cavern" from *Tarka the Otter* by Henry Williamson.

William Heinemann Ltd., Laurence Pollinger Ltd., and the estate of the late Mrs. Frieda Lawrence, for "Adolf" from *Phoenix* by D. H. Lawrence.

David Attenborough Esq., for "Python up a Tree" from *Zoo Quest for a Dragon* by David Attenborough, published by Lutterworth Press.

Oxford University Press, for "The Thak Man-Eater" from *The Man-Eaters of Kumaon* by Jim Corbett.

Curtis Brown Ltd., and Gerald Durrell Esq., for "The Chessboard Fields" from *My Family and Other Animals* by Gerald Durrell.

ACKNOWLEDGEMENTS

David Stephen Esq., for "The Laird and the Fawn" from *Six-Pointer Buck* by David Stephen, published by Lutterworth Press.

Mrs. George Bambridge, Macmillan of London & Basingstoke, and A. P. Watt & Son, for "Kaa's Hunting" from *The Jungle Book* by Rudyard Kipling.

Helen W. Thurber, Rosemary Thurber Sauers and Harper & Row, New York, for "Snapshot of a Dog" from *The Thurber Carnival*. (Copyright © 1945 James Thurber, copyright © 1973 Helen W. Thurber and Rosemary Thurber Sauers; originally printed in *The New Yorker*.)

Harper & Row, New York, for "The Dog that Bit People" from *My Life and Hard Times* by James Thurber. (Copyright © 1933, 1961 James Thurber.)

Contents

CONTENTS

Introduction

MANY THOUSANDS of animal stories have been written by a great variety of authors, so that when you are asked, quite suddenly, to pick thirteen of the ones you like best you are in a bit of a quandary, and thirteen seems a very inadequate amount.

Animal stories by and large fall into four categories: The first, and by far the most difficult to write, is the story in which the author tries to imagine he is the animal, reporting everything from the creature's point of view, but without turning the animal into a sort of furry human being. The past master of this is, of course, Henry Williamson. The extract from *Tarka the Otter* that I have chosen will, I think, show you how Henry Williamson literally *became* an Otter in his writing, and achieved this without making the animal talk or otherwise behave in a human fashion.

The second type of animal story is the one where the author describes an exciting incident with an animal, whether in hunting it or trying to catch it. These stories vary, some being written in a very straightforward and slightly humorous fashion, such as Arthur Grimble's "Assignment with an Octopus", and David Attenborough's "Python up a Tree", or in a rather rich and poetic manner, like the style of Herman Melville in his wonderful description of the great shoal of whales or T. H. White in his brilliant description of the wild boar hunt.

Thirdly, there are the humorous animal stories, and in

this field there are very few people who can touch James Thurber. He describes his animals whimsically, with great humour, but never sentimentalizes them too much; if "The Dog that Bit People" does not leave you chuckling I shall be very surprised.

Now the fourth category of animal story is the one where the author deliberately makes his animals talk and think like human beings, but still behave like animals. A lot of people do not like this type of story, because they say it is wrong to attribute human thought and speech to animals. I think this is stupid, because, providing the author still makes his animals behave as they would do in the wild state, I see no harm in letting them communicate with each other in human speech. Rudyard Kipling is the great exponent of this type of story, and I think you will find "Kaa's Hunting" one of the most exciting bits from *The First Jungle Book*.

Many of the pieces that I have chosen here are, of course, only extracts from full-length books. But I hope they are sufficiently interesting to make you want to read the whole of the book. For example, both *Tarka the Otter* and *Moby Dick* are not only very exciting books but are filled with the most astonishing and accurate information about natural history in general, and are beautifully written.

I hope you will enjoy my choice, and that it will encourage you to explore the vast field of Animal Stories for the many other stories there are to be found.

Gerald Durrell.

1 *Snapshot of a Dog*

JAMES THURBER

I RAN ACROSS a dim photograph of him the other day, going through some old things. He's been dead twenty-five years. His name was Rex (my two brothers and I named him when we were in our early teens) and he was a bull terrier. "An American bull terrier," we used to say proudly; none of your English bulls. He had one brindle eye that sometimes made him look like a clown and sometimes reminded you of a politician with derby hat and cigar. The rest of him was white except for a brindle saddle that always seemed to be slipping off and a brindle stocking on a hind leg.

Nevertheless, there was a nobility about him. He was big and muscular and beautifully made. He never lost his dignity even when trying to accomplish the extravagant tasks my brothers and myself used to set for him. One of these was the bringing of a ten-foot wooden rail into the yard through the back gate. We would throw it out into the alley and tell him to go get it. Rex was as powerful as a wrestler, and there were not many things that he couldn't manage somehow to get hold of with his great jaws and lift or drag to wherever he wanted to put them, or wherever we wanted them put. He could catch the rail at the balance and lift it clear of the ground and trot with great confidence towards the gate. Of course, since the gate was only four feet wide or so, he couldn't bring the rail in broadside. He found that out when he got a few terrific jolts, but he wouldn't give up. He finally figured out how to do it, by dragging the rail, holding on to one end, growling. He got a great, wagging satisfaction out of his work. We used to bet kids who had never seen Rex in action that he could catch a baseball thrown as high as they could throw it. He almost never let us down. Rex could hold a baseball with ease in his mouth, in one cheek, as if it were a chew of tobacco.

He was a tremendous fighter, but he never started fights. I don't believe he liked to get into them, despite the fact that he came from a line of fighters. He never went for another dog's throat, but for one of its ears (that teaches a dog a lesson), and he would get his grip, close his eyes, and hold on. He could hold on for hours. His longest fight lasted from dusk until almost pitch-dark, one Sunday. It was fought in East Main Street in Columbus with a large, snarly nondescript that belonged to a big coloured man. When Rex finally got his ear grip the brief whirlwind of snarling turned to screeching. It was frightening to listen to and to watch. The Negro boldly picked the dogs up somehow and began swinging them round his head, and finally let them fly like a hammer throw, but although they landed ten feet away with a great plump, Rex still held on.

The two dogs eventually worked their way to the middle of the car tracks, and after a while two or three street-cars were held up by the fight. A motorman tried to pry Rex's jaws open with a switch rod; somebody lighted a fire and made a torch of a stick and held that to Rex's tail, but he paid no attention. In the end, all the residents and storekeepers in the neighbourhood were on hand, shouting this, suggesting that. Rex's joy of battle, when battle was joined, was almost tranquil. He had a kind of pleasant expression during fights, not a vicious one, his eyes closed in what would have seemed to be sleep had it not been for the turmoil of the struggle. The Oak Street Fire Department finally had to be sent for—I don't know why nobody thought of it sooner. Five or six pieces of apparatus arrived, followed by a battalion chief. A hose was attached and a powerful stream of water was turned on the dogs. Rex held on for several moments more while the torrent buffeted him about like a log in a freshet. He was a hundred yards away from where the fight started when he finally let go.

The story of that Homeric fight got all around town, and some of our relatives looked upon the incident as a blot on the family name. They insisted that we get rid of

Rex, but we were very happy with him, and nobody could have made us give him up. We would have left town with him first, along any road there was to go. It would have been different, perhaps, if he'd ever started fights, or looked for trouble. But he had a gentle disposition. He never bit a person in the ten strenuous years that he lived, nor even growled at anyone except prowlers. He killed cats, that is true, but quickly and neatly and without especial malice, the way men kill certain animals. It was the only thing he did that we could never cure him of doing. He never killed, or even chased, a squirrel. I don't know why. He had his own philosophy about such things. He never ran barking after wagons or automobiles. He didn't seem to see the idea in pursuing something you couldn't catch, or something you couldn't do anything with, even if you did catch it. A wagon was one of the things he couldn't tug along with his mighty jaws, and he knew it. Wagons, therefore, were not a part of his world.

Swimming was his favourite recreation. The first time he ever saw a body of water (Alum Creek), he trotted nervously along the steep bank for a while, fell to barking wildly, and finally plunged in from a height of eight feet or more. I shall always remember that shining, virgin dive. Then he swam upstream and back just for the pleasure of it, like a man. It was fun to see him battle upstream against a stiff current, struggling and growling every foot of the way. He had as much fun in the water as any person I have known. You didn't have to throw a stick in the water to get him to go in. Of course, he would bring back a stick to you if you did throw one in. He would even have brought back a piano if you had thrown one in.

That reminds me of the night, way after midnight, when he went a-roving in the light of the moon and brought back a small chest of drawers that he found somewhere—how far from the house nobody ever knew; since it was Rex, it could easily have been half a mile. There were no drawers in the chest when he got it home, and it wasn't a good one—he hadn't taken it out of anybody's house; it was just an old cheap piece that somebody had abandoned on a trash heap. Still, it was something he wanted, probably because it presented a nice problem in transportation. It tested his mettle. We first knew about his achievement when, deep in the night, we heard him trying to get the chest up on to the porch. It sounded as if two or three people were trying to tear the house down. We came downstairs and turned on the porch light. Rex was on the top step trying to pull the thing up, but it had caught somehow and he was just holding his own till dawn if we hadn't helped him. The next day we carted the chest miles away and threw it out. If we had thrown it out in a nearby alley he would have brought it home again, as a small token of his integrity in such matters. After all, he had been taught to carry heavy wooden objects about, and he was proud of his prowess.

I am glad Rex never saw a trained police dog jump. He was just an amateur jumper himself, but the most daring and tenacious I have ever seen. He would take on any fence we pointed out to him. Six feet was easy for him, and he could do eight by making a tremendous leap and hauling himself over finally by his paws, grunting and straining; but he lived and died without knowing that twelve- and sixteen-foot walls were too much for him. Frequently, after letting him try to go over one for a while, we would have to carry him home. He would never have given up trying.

There was in his world no such thing as the impossible. Even death couldn't beat him down. He died, it is true, but only, as one of his admirers said, after "straight-arming the death angel" for more than an hour. Late one afternoon he wandered home, too slowly and too uncertainly to be the Rex that had trotted briskly homeward up our avenue for ten years. I think we all knew when he came through the gate that he was dying. He had apparently taken a terrible beating, probably from the owner of some dog that he had got into a fight with. His head and body were scarred. His heavy collar with the teeth marks of many a battle on it was awry; some of the big brass studs in it were sprung loose from the leather. He licked at our hands and, staggering, fell, but got up again. We could see that he was looking for someone. One of his three masters was not home. He did not get home for an hour. During that hour the bull terrier fought against death as he had fought against the cold strong current of Alum Creek, as he had fought to climb twelve-foot walls. When the person he was waiting for did come through the gate, whistling, ceasing to whistle, Rex walked a few wobbly paces towards him, touched his hand with his muzzle, and fell down again. This time he didn't get up.

2 *Assignment with an Octopus*

ARTHUR GRIMBLE

I CERTAINLY SHOULD never have ventured out alone for pure sport, armed with nothing but a knife, to fight a tiger-shark in its own element. I am as little ashamed of that degree of discretion as the big-game hunter who takes care not to attack a rhinoceros with a shotgun. The fear I had for the larger kinds of octopus was quite different. It was a blind fear, sick with disgust, unreasoned as a child's horror of darkness. Victor Hugo was the man who first brought it up to the level of my conscious thought. I still remember vividly the impression left on me as a boy of fourteen by that account in *Les*

Travailleurs de la Mer of Gilliatt's fight with the monster that caught him among the rocks of The Douvres. For years after reading it, I tortured myself with wondering how ever I could behave with decent courage if faced with a giant at once so strong and so loathsome. My commonest nightmare of the period was of an octopus-like Presence poised motionless behind me, towards which I dared not turn, from which my limbs were too frozen to escape. But that phase did pass before I left school, and the Thing lay dormant inside me until a day at Tarawa.

Before I reached Tarawa, however, chance gave me a swift glimpse of what a biggish octopus can do to a man. I was wading at low tide one calm evening on the lip of the reef at Ocean Island when a Baanaban villager, back from fishing, brought his canoe to land within twenty yards of where I stood. There was no more than a show of breaking seas, but the water was only knee deep, and this obliged the fisherman to slide overboard and handle his lightened craft over the jagged edge. But no sooner were his feet upon the reef than he seemed to be tied where he stood. The canoe was washed shorewards ahead of him; while he stood with legs braced, tugging desperately away from something. I had just time to see a tapering, greyish-yellow rope curled around his right wrist before he broke away from it. He fell sprawling into the foam at the reef's edge. The fisherman picked himself up and nursed his right arm. I had reached him by then. The octopus had caught him with only the tip of one tentacle, but the terrible hold of the few suckers on his wrist had torn the skin whole from it as he wrenched himself adrift.

Possibly, if you can watch objectively, the sight of

Octopus Vulgaris searching for crabs and crayfish on the floor of the lagoon may move you to something like admiration. You cannot usually see the dreadful eyes from a water-glass straight above its feeding-ground, and your feeling for crustaceans is too impersonal for horror at their fates between pouncing suckers and jaws. There is real beauty in the rich change of its colours as it moves from shadow to sunlight, and the gliding ease of its arms as they reach and flicker over the rough rocks fascinates the eye with its deadly grace. You feel that if only the creature would stick to its grubbing on the bottom the shocking ugliness of its shape might even win your sympathy, as for some poor Caliban in the enchanted garden of the lagoon. But it is no honest grubber in the open. For every one of its kind that you see crawling below you, there are a dozen skulking in recesses of the reef that falls away like a cliff from the edge where you stand watching. When *Octopus Vulgaris* has eaten its fill of the teeming crabs and crayfish it seeks a dark cleft in the coral face and anchors itself there with a few of the large suckers nearest to its body. Thus shielded from attack in the rear, with tentacles gathered to pounce, it squats glaring from the shadows, alert for anything alive to swim within striking distance. It can hurl one or all of those whiplashes forward with the speed of dark lightning, and once its scores of suckers, rimmed with hooks for grip on slippery skins, are clamped about their prey, nothing but the brute's death will break their awful hold.

But that very quality of the octopus that most horrifies the imagination, its relentless tenacity, becomes its undoing when hungry man steps into the picture. The Gilbertese happen to value certain parts of it as food, and their method of fighting it is coolly based upon the one fact that its arms never change their grip. They hunt for it in pairs. One man acts as the bait, his partner as the killer. First, they swim eyes-under at low tide just off the reef, and search the crannies of the submarine cliff for sight of any tentacle that may flicker out for a catch. When they have placed their quarry they land on the reef for the next stage. The human bait starts the real game. He dives and tempts the lurking brute by swimming a few strokes in front of its cranny, at first a little beyond striking range. Then he turns and makes straight for the cranny, to give himself into the embrace of those waiting arms. Sometimes nothing happens. The beast will not always respond to the lure. But usually it strikes.

The partner on the reef above stares down through the pellucid water, waiting for his moment. His teeth are his only weapon. His killing efficiency depends on his avoiding every one of those strangling arms. He must wait until his partner's body has been drawn right up to the entrance of the cleft. The monster inside is groping then with its horny mouth against the victim's flesh, and sees nothing beyond it. That point is reached in a matter of no more than thirty seconds after the decoy has plunged. The killer dives, lays hold of his pinioned friend at arms' length, and jerks him away from the cleft; the octopus is torn adrift from the anchorage of its proximal suckers, and clamps itself the more fiercely to its prey. In the same second the human bait gives a kick which brings him, with quarry annexed, to the surface. He turns on his back, still holding his breath for better buoyancy, and this exposes the body of the beast for the kill. The killer closes in, grasps the evil head from behind, and wrenches it away from its meal. Turning the face up towards himself, he plunges his teeth between the bulging eyes, and bites down and in with all his strength. That is the end of it. It dies on the instant; the suckers release their hold; the arms fall away; the two fishers paddle with whoops of delighted laughter to the reef, where they string the catch to a pole before going to rout out the next one.

Any two boys of seventeen, any day of the week, will go out and get you half a dozen octopus like that for the mere fun of it. Here lies the whole point of this story. The hunt is, in the most literal sense, nothing but child's play to the Gilbertese.

As I was standing one day at the end of a jetty in Tarawa lagoon, I saw two boys from the near village shouldering a string of octopus slung on a pole between them. I started to wade out in their direction, but before I hailed them they had stopped, planted the carrying-pole upright in a fissure and, leaving it there, swam off the edge for a while with faces submerged, evidently searching for something under the water. I had only been a few months at Tarawa, and that was my first near view of an octopus-hunt. I watched every stage of it from the dive of the human bait to the landing of the dead catch. When it was over I went up to them. I could hardly believe that in those few seconds, with no more than a frivolous-looking splash or two on the surface, they could have found, caught, and killed the creature they were now stringing up before my eyes. They explained the amusing simplicity of the thing.

"There's only one trick the decoy-man must never forget," they said, "and that's not difficult to remember. If he is not wearing the water-spectacles of the Men of Matang he must cover his eyes with a hand as he comes close to the *kika* (octopus), or the suckers might blind him." It appears that the ultimate fate of the eyes was not the thing to worry about; the immediate point was that the sudden pain of a sucker clamping itself to an eyeball might cause the bait to expel his breath and inhale sea-water; that would spoil his buoyancy, and he would fail then to give his friend the best chance of a kill.

Then they began whispering together. I knew in a curdling flash what they were saying to each other. Before they turned to speak to me again, a horrified conviction was upon me. My wretched curiosity had led me into a trap from which there was no escape. They were going to propose that I should take a turn at being the bait myself, just to see how delightfully easy it was. And that is what they did. It did not even occur to them that I might not leap at the offer. I was already known as a young Man of Matang who liked swimming, and fishing, and laughing with the villagers; I had just shown an interest in this particular form of hunting; naturally, I should enjoy the fun of it as much as they did. Without even waiting for my answer, they gleefully ducked off the edge of the reef to look for another octopus—a fine fat one—*mine*.

I was dressed in khaki slacks, canvas shoes, and a short-sleeved singlet. I took off the shoes and made up my mind to shed the singlet if told to do so; but I was wildly determined to stick to my trousers throughout. Dead or alive, said a voice within me, an official minus his pants is a preposterous object, and I felt I could not face that extra horror. However, nobody asked me to remove anything.

I hope I did not look as yellow as I felt when I stood to take the plunge; I have never been so sick with fear before or since. "Remember, one hand for your eyes," said someone from a thousand miles off, and I dived.

I do not suppose it is really true that the eyes of an octopus shine in the dark, besides, it was clear daylight only six feet down in the limpid water; but I could have sworn the brute's eyes burned at me as I turned in towards his cranny. That dark glow—whatever may have been its origin—was the last thing I saw as I blacked out with my left hand and rose into his clutches. Then I remember chiefly a dreadful sliminess with a herculean power behind it. Something whipped round my left forearm and the back of my neck, binding the two together. In the same flash another something slapped itself high on my forehead, and I felt it crawling down inside the back of my singlet. My impulse was to tear at it with my right hand, but I felt the whole of that arm pinioned to my ribs.

In most emergencies the mind works with crystal-clear impersonality. This was not even an emergency, for I knew myself perfectly safe. But my boyhood's nightmare was upon me. When I felt the swift constriction of those disgusting arms jerk my head and shoulders in towards the reef, my mind went blank of every thought save the beastliness of contact with that squat head. A mouth began to nuzzle below my throat, at the junction of the collar-bones. I forgot there was anyone to save me. Yet something still directed me to hold my breath.

I was awakened from my cowardly trance by a quick, strong pull on my shoulders, back from the cranny. The cables around me tightened painfully, but I knew I was adrift from the reef. I gave a kick, rose to the surface, and turned on my back with the brute sticking out of my chest like a tumour. My mouth was smothered by some flabby moving horror. The suckers felt like hot rings pulling at my skin. It was only two seconds, I suppose, from then to the attack of my deliverer, but it seemed like a century of nausea.

My friend came up between me and the reef. He pounced, pulled, bit down, and the thing was over—for everyone but me. At the sudden relaxation of the tentacles, I let out a great breath, sank, and drew in the next under water. It took the united help of both boys to get me, coughing, heaving, and pretending to join in their delighted laughter, back to the reef. I had to submit there to a kind of war-dance round me, in which the dead beast was slung whizzing past my head from one to the other. I had a chance to observe then that it was not by any stretch of fancy a giant, but just plain average. That took the bulge out of my budding self-esteem. I left hurriedly for the cover of the jetty, and was sick.

3 *The Boar Hunt*

T. H. WHITE

THE WART got up early next morning. He made a determined effort the moment he woke, threw off the great bearskin rug under which he slept, and plunged his body into the biting air. He dressed furiously, trembling, skipping about to keep warm, and hissing blue breaths to himself as if he were grooming a horse. He broke the ice in a basin and dipped his face in it with a grimace like eating something sour, said A-a-ah, and rubbed his stinging cheeks vigorously with a towel. Then he felt quite warm again and scampered off to the emergency kennels, to watch the King's huntsman making his last arrangements.

Master William Twyti turned out in daylight to be a shrivelled, harassed-looking man, with an expression of melancholy on his face. All his life he had been forced to pursue various animals for the royal table, and, when he had caught them, to cut them up into proper joints. He was more than half a butcher. He had to know what parts the hounds should eat, and what parts should be given to his assistants. He had to cut everything up handsomely, leaving two vertebrae on the tail to make the chine look attractive, and almost ever since he could remember he had been either pursuing a hart or cutting it up into helpings.

He was not particularly fond of doing this. The harts and hinds in their herds, the boars in their singulars, the skulks of foxes, the richesses of martens, the bevies of roes, the cetes of badgers, and the routs of wolves—all came to him more or less as something which you either skinned or flayed and then took home to cook. You could talk to him about os and argos, suet and grease, croteys, fewmets and fiants, but he only looked polite. He knew that you were showing off your knowledge of these words, which were to him a business. You could talk about a mighty boar which had nearly slashed you last winter, but he only stared at you with his distant eyes. He had been slashed sixteen times by mighty boars, and his legs had white weals of shiny flesh that stretched right up to his ribs. While you talked, he got on with whatever part of his profession he had in hand. There was only one thing which could move Master William Twyti. Summer or winter, snow or shine, he was running or galloping after boars and harts, and all the time his soul was somewhere else. Mention a *hare* to Master Twyti and, although he would still go on galloping after the wretched hart which seemed to be his destiny, he would gallop with one eye over his shoulder yearning for puss. It was the only thing he ever talked about. He was always being sent to one castle or another, all over England, and when he was there the local servants would fête him and keep his glass filled and ask him about his greatest hunts. He would answer distractedly in monosyllables. But if anybody mentioned a huske of hares he was all attention, and then he would thump his glass upon the table and discourse upon the marvels of this astonishing beast, declaring that you could never blow a menee for it, because the same hare could at one time be male and another time female, while it carried grease and croteyed and gnawed, which things no beast in the earth did except it.

Wart watched the great man in silence for some time, then went indoors to see if there was any hope of breakfast. He found that there was, for the whole castle was suffering from the same sort of nervous excitement which had got him out of bed so early, and even Merlyn had dressed himself in a pair of breeches which had been fashionable some centuries later with the University Beagles.

Boar-hunting was fun. It was nothing like badger-digging or covert-shooting or fox-hunting today. Perhaps the nearest thing to it would be ferreting for rabbits—except that you used dogs instead of ferrets, had a boar that easily might kill you, instead of a rabbit, and carried a boar-spear upon which your life depended instead of a gun. They did not usually hunt the boar on horseback. Perhaps the reason for this was that the boar season happened in the two winter months, when the old English snow would be liable to ball in your horse's hoofs and render galloping too dangerous. The result was that you were yourself on foot, armed only with steel, against an adversary who weighed a good deal more than you did and who could unseam you from the nave to the chaps, and set your head upon his battlements. There was only one rule in boar-hunting. It was: Hold on. If the boar charged, you had to drop on one knee and present your boar-spear in his direction. You held the butt of it with your right hand on the ground to take the shock, while you stretched your left arm to its fullest extent and kept the point towards the charging boar. The spear was as sharp as a razor, and it had a cross-piece about eighteen inches away from the point. This cross-piece or horizontal bar prevented the spear from going more than eighteen inches into his chest. Without the cross-piece, a charging boar would have been capable of rushing right up the spear, even if it did go through him, and getting at the hunter like that. But with the cross-piece he was held away from you at a spear's length, with eighteen inches of steel inside him. It was in this situation that you had to hold on.

He weighed between ten and twenty score, and his one object in life was to heave and weave and sidestep, until he could get at his assailant and champ him into chops, while the assailant's one object was not to let go of the spear, clasped tight under his arm, until somebody had come to finish him off. If he could keep hold of his end of the weapon, while the other end was stuck in the boar, he knew that there was at least a spear's length between them, however much the boar ran him round the forest. You may be able to understand, if you think this over, why all the sportsmen of the castle got up early for the Boxing Day Meet, and ate their breakfast with a certain amount of suppressed feeling.

"Ah," said Sir Grummore, gnawing a pork chop which he held in his fingers, "down in time for breakfast, hey?"

"Yes, I am," said the Wart.

"Fine huntin' mornin'," said Sir Grummore. "Got your spear sharp, hey?"

"Yes, I have, thank you," said the Wart. He went over to the sideboard to get a chop for himself.

"Come on, Pellinore," said Sir Ector. "Have a few of these chickens. You're eatin' nothin' this mornin'."

King Pellinore said, "I don't think I will, thank you all the same. I don't think I feel quite the thing, this morning, what?"

Sir Grummore took his nose out of his chop and inquired sharply, "Nerves?"

"Oh, no," cried King Pellinore. "Oh, no, really not that, what? I think I must have taken something last night that disagreed with me."

"Nonsense, my dear fellah," said Sir Ector, "here you are, just you have a few chickens to keep your strength up."

He helped the unfortunate King to two or three capons, and the latter sat down miserably at the end of the table, trying to swallow a few bits of them.

"Need them," said Sir Grummore meaningly, "by the end of the day, I dare say."

"Do you think so?"

"Know so," said Sir Grummore, and winked at his host.

The Wart noticed that Sir Ector and Sir Grummore were eating with rather exaggerated gusto. He did not feel that he could manage more than one chop himself, and, as for Kay, he had stayed away from the breakfast-room altogether.

When breakfast was over, and Master Twyti had been consulted, the Boxing Day cavalcade moved off to the Meet. Perhaps the hounds would have seemed rather a mixed pack to a master of hounds today. There were half a dozen black-and-white alaunts, which looked like greyhounds with the heads of bull-terriers or worse. These, which were the proper hounds for boars, wore muzzles because of their ferocity. The gaze-hounds, of which there were two taken just in case, were in reality nothing but greyhounds according to modern language, while the lymers were a sort of mixture between the blood-hound and the red setter of today. The latter had collars on, and were led with straps. The braches were like beagles, and trotted along with the master in the way that beagles always have trotted, and a charming way it is.

With the hounds went the foot-people. Merlyn, in his running breeches, looked rather like Lord Baden-Powell, except, of course, that the latter did not wear a beard. Sir Ector was dressed in "sensible" leather clothes—it was not considered sporting to hunt in armour—and he walked beside Master Twyti with that bothered and important expression which has always been worn by masters of hounds. Sir Grummore, just behind, was puffing and asking everybody whether they had sharpened their spears. King Pellinore had dropped back among the villagers, feeling that there was safety in numbers. All the villagers were there, every male soul on the estate from Hob the austringer down to old Wat with no nose, every man carrying a spear or a pitchfork or a worn scythe blade on a stout pole. Even some of the young women who were courting had come out, with baskets of provisions for the men. It was a regular Boxing Day Meet.

At the edge of the forest the last follower joined up. He was a tall, distinguished looking person dressed in green, and he carried a seven foot bow.

"Good morning, Master," he said pleasantly to Sir Ector.

"Ah, yes," said Sir Ector. "Yes, yes, good mornin', eh? Yes, good mornin'."

He led the gentleman in green aside and said in a loud whisper that could be heard by everybody, "For heaven's sake, my dear fellow, do be careful. This is the King's own huntsman, and those two other chaps are King Pellinore and Sir Grummore. Now do be a good chap, my dear fellow, and don't say anything controversial, will you, old boy, there's a good chap?"

"Certainly I won't," said the green man reassuringly, "but I think you had better introduce me to them."

Sir Ector blushed deeply, and called out, "Ah, Grummore, come over here a minute, will you? I want to introduce a friend of mine, old chap, a chap called Wood, old chap—Wood with a W, you know, not an H. Yes, and this is King Pellinore. Master Wood—King Pelli-nore."

"Hail," said King Pellinore, who had not quite got out of the habit when nervous.

"How do?" said Sir Grummore. "No relation to Robin Hood, I suppose?"

"Oh, not in the least," interrupted Sir Ector hastily. "Double you, double owe, dee, you know, like the stuff they make furniture out of—furniture, you know, and spears, and—well—spears, you know, and furniture."

"How do you do?" said Robin.

"Hail," said King Pellinore.

"Well," said Sir Grummore, "it is funny you should both wear green."

"Yes, it is funny, isn't it?" said Sir Ector anxiously. "He wears it in mournin' for an aunt of his, who died by fallin' out of a tree."

"Beg pardon, I'm sure," said Sir Grummore, grieved at having touched upon this tender subject—and all was well.

"Now, then, Mr. Wood," said Sir Ector when he had recovered. "Where shall we go for our first draw?"

As soon as this question had been put, Master Twyti was fetched into the conversation, and a brief confabula-tion followed in which all sorts of technical terms like "lesses" were bandied about. Then there was a long walk in the wintry forest, and the fun began.

Wart had lost the panicky feeling which had taken hold of his stomach when he was breaking his fast. The exercise and the snow-wind had breathed him, so that his eyes sparkled almost as brilliantly as the frost crystals in

the white winter sunlight, and his blood raced with the
excitement of the chase. He watched the lymerer who
held the two bloodhound dogs on their leashes, and saw
the dogs straining more and more as the boar's lair was
approached. He saw how, one by one and ending with
the gaze-hounds—who did not hunt by scent—the various
hounds became uneasy and began to whimper with desire.
He noticed Robin pause and pick up some lesses, which
he handed to Master Twyti, and then the whole cavalcade came to a halt. They had reached the dangerous
spot.

Boar-hunting was like cub-hunting to this extent, that
the boar was attempted to be held up. The object of the
hunt was to kill him as quickly as possible. Wart took up
his position in the circle round the monster's lair, and
knelt down on one knee in the snow, with the handle of his
spear couched on the ground, ready for emergencies. He
felt the hush which fell upon the company, and saw
Master Twyti wave silently to the lymerer to uncouple
his hounds. The two lymers plunged immediately into
the covert which the hunters surrounded. They ran
mute.

There were five long minutes during which nothing
happened. The hearts beat thunderously in the circle, and
a small vein on the side of each neck throbbed in harmony
with each heart. The heads turned quickly from side to
side, as each man assured himself of his neighbours, and
the breath of life steamed away on the north wind sweetly,
as each realized how beautiful life was, which a reeking
tusk might, in a few seconds, rape away from one or
another of them if things went wrong.

The boar did not express his fury with his voice. There was no uproar in the covert or yelping from the lymers. Only, about a hundred yards away from the Wart, there was suddenly a black creature standing on the edge of the clearing. It did not seem to be a boar particularly, not in the first seconds that it stood there. It had come too quickly to seem to be anything. It was charging Sir Grummore before the Wart had recognized what it was.

The black thing rushed over the white snow, throwing up little puffs of it. Sir Grummore—also looking black against the snow—turned a quick somersault in a larger puff. A kind of grunt, but no noise of falling, came clearly on the north wind, and then the boar was gone. When it was gone, but not before, the Wart knew certain things about it—things which he had not had time to notice while the boar was there. He remembered the rank mane of bristles standing upright on its razor back, one flash of a sour tush, the staring ribs, the head held low, and the red flame from a piggy eye.

Sir Grummore got up, dusting snow out of himself unhurt, blaming his spear. A few drops of blood were to be seen frothing on the white earth. Master Twyti put his horn to his lips. The alaunts were uncoupled as the exciting notes of the menee began to ring through the forest, and then the whole scene began to move. The lymers which had reared the boar—the proper word for dislodging—were allowed to pursue him to make them keen on their work. The braches gave musical tongue. The alaunts galloped baying through the drifts. Everybody began to shout and run.

"Avoy, avoy!" cried the foot-people. "Shahou, shahou! Avaunt, sire, avaunt!"

"Swef, swef!" cried Master Twyti anxiously. "Now, now, gentlemen, give the hounds room, if you please."

"I say, I say!" cried King Pellinore. "Did anybody see which way he went? What an exciting day, what? Sa sa cy avaunt, cy sa avaunt, sa cy avaunt!"

"Hold hard, Pellinore!" cried Sir Ector. "'Ware, hounds, man, 'ware hounds. Can't catch him yourself, you know. Il est hault. Il est hault!"

And "Til est ho," echoed the foot-people. "Tilly-ho," sang the trees. "Tally-ho," murmured the distant snow-drifts as the heavy branches, disturbed by the vibrations, slid noiseless puffs of sparkling powder to the muffled earth.

The Wart found himself running with Master Twyti.

It was like beagling in a way, except that it was beagling in a forest where it was sometimes difficult even to move. Everything depended on the music of the hounds and the various notes which the huntsman could blow to tell where he was and what he was doing. Without these the whole field would have been lost in two minutes—and even with them about half of it was lost in three.

Wart stuck to Twyti like a burr. He could move as quickly as the huntsman because, although the latter had the experience of a life-time, he himself was smaller to get through obstacles and had, moreover, been taught by Maid Marian. He noticed that Robin kept up too, but soon the grunting of Sir Ector and the baa-ing of King Pellinore were left behind. Sir Grummore had given in early, having had most of the breath knocked out of him by the boar, and stood far in the rear declaring that his spear could no longer be quite sharp. Kay had stayed with him, so that he should not get lost. The foot-people had been early mislaid because they did not understand the notes of the horn. Merlyn had torn his breeches and stopped to mend them up by magic.

The sergeant had thrown out his chest so far in crying Tally-ho and telling everybody which way they ought to run that he had lost all sense of place, and was leading a disconsolate party of villagers, in Indian file, at the double, with knees up, in the wrong direction. Hob was still in the running.

"Swef, swef," panted the huntsman, addressing the Wart as if he had been a hound. "Not so fast, master, they are going off the line."

Even as he spoke, Wart noticed that the hound music was weaker and more querulous.

"Stop," said Robin, "or we may tumble over him."

The music died away.

"Swef, swef!" shouted Master Twyti at the top of his voice. "Sto arere, so howe, so howe!" He swung his baldrick in front of him, and, lifting the horn to his lips, began to blow a recheat.

There was a single note from one of the lymers.

"Hoo arere," cried the huntsman.

The lymer's note grew in confidence, faltered, then rose to the full bay.

"Hoo arere! Here how, amy. Hark to Beaumont the valiant! Ho moy, ho moy, hole, hole, hole, hole."

The lymer was taken up by the tenor bells of the braches. The noises grew to a crescendo of excitement as the blood-thirsty thunder of the alaunts pealed through the lesser notes.

"They have him," said Twyti briefly, and the three humans began to run again, while the huntsman blew encouragement with Trou-rou-root.

In a small bushment the grimly boar stood at bay. He had got his hindquarters into the nook of a tree blown down by a gale, in an impregnable position. He stood on the defensive with his upper lip writhed back in a snarl. The blood of Sir Grummore's gash welled fatly among the bristles of his shoulder and down his leg, while the foam of his chops dropped on the blushing snow and melted it. His small eyes darted in every direction. The hounds stood round, yelling at his mask, and Beaumont, with his back broken, writhed at his feet. He paid no further attention to the living hound, which could do him no harm. He was black, flaming, and bloody.

"So-ho," said the huntsman.

He advanced with his spear held in front of him, and the hounds, encouraged by their master, stepped forward with him pace by pace.

The scene changed as suddenly as a house of cards falling down. The boar was not at bay any more, but charging Master Twyti. As it charged, the alaunts closed in, seizing it fiercely by the shoulder or throat or leg, so that what surged down on the huntsman was not one boar but a bundle of animals. He dared not use his spear for fear of hurting the dogs. The bundle rolled forward unchecked, as if the hounds did not impede it at all. Twyti began to reverse his spear, to keep the charge off with its butt end, but even as he reversed it the tussle was upon him. He sprang back, tripped over a root, and the battle closed on top. The Wart pranced round the edge, waving his own spear in an agony, but there was nowhere where he dared to thrust it in. Robin dropped his spear, drew his falchion in the same movement, stepped into the huddle of snarls, and calmly picked an alaunt up by the leg. The dog did not let go, but there was space where its body had been. Into this space the falchion went slowly, once, twice, thrice. The whole super-structure stumbled, recovered itself, stumbled again, and sank down ponderously on its left side. The hunt was over.

Master Twyti drew one leg slowly from under the boar, stood up, took hold of his knee with his right hand, moved it inquiringly in various directions, nodded to himself and stretched his back straight. Then he picked up his spear without saying anything and limped over to Beaumont. He knelt down beside him and took his head on his lap. He stroked Beaumont's head and said, "Hark to Beaumont. Softly, Beaumont, mon amy. Oyez a Beaumont the valiant. Swef, le douce Beaumont, swef, swef." Beaumont licked his hand but could not wag his tail. The huntsman nodded to Robin, who was standing behind, and held the hound's eyes with his own. He said "Good dog, Beaumont the valiant, sleep now, old friend Beaumont, good old dog." Then Robin's falchion let Beaumont out of this world, to run free with Orion and roll among the stars.

The Wart did not like to watch Master Twyti for a moment. The strange, leathery man stood up without saying anything and whipped the hounds off the corpse of the boar as he was accustomed to do. He put his horn to his lips and blew the four long notes of the mort without a quaver. But he was blowing the notes for a different reason, and he startled the Wart because he seemed to be crying.

4 *Seal Cavern*

HENRY WILLIAMSON

THE TREES of the riverside wept their last dry tears, and the mud in the tidehead pool made them heavy and black; and after a fresh, when salmon came over the bar, beginning their long journey to spawn in the gravel where the rivers ran young and bright, broken black fragments were strewn on the banks and ridges of the wide estuary. In November the poplars were like bedraggled gull-feathers stuck in the ground, except for one or two or three leaves which fluttered on their tops throughout the gales of November.

One evening, when the ebb-tide was leaning the channel buoys to the west and the gulls were flying silent and low over the sea to the darkening cliffs of the headland, Tarka and Greymuzzle set out on a journey. They had followed the salmon up the river, and Greymuzzle had returned for a purpose. The bright eye of the light-house, standing like a bleached bone at the edge of the sandhills, blinked in the clear air. The otters were carried down amidst swirls and topplings of waves in the wake of a ketch, while the mumble of the bar grew in their ears. Beyond the ragged horizon of grey breakers the day had gone, clouded and dull, leaving a purplish pallor on the cold sea.

The waves slid and rose under the masted ship, pushing the white surge of the bar from her bows. A crest rolled under her keel and she pitched into a trough. On the left a mist arose off a bank of grey boulders, on which a destroyer lay broken and sea-scattered. It had lain there for years, in bits like beetle fragments in a gorse-spider's grey web-tunnel. One of the great seas that drive the flying spume over the potwallopers' grazing marsh had thrown it up on the Pebble Ridge. During the day Tarka and Greymuzzle had slept under the rusty plates, curled warm on the wave-worn boulders rolled there by the seas along Hercules Promontory.

Two hours after midnight the otters had swum five miles along the shallow coast and had reached the cave of the headland, which Greymuzzle had remembered when she had felt her young kick inside her. The tide left deep pools among the rocks, which the otters searched for blennies and gobies, and other little fish which lurked under the seaweed. They caught prawns, which were eaten tail first, but the heads were never swallowed. With their teeth they tore mussels off the rocks, and holding them in their paws, they cracked them and licked out the fish. While Greymuzzle was digging out a sand-eel, Tarka explored a deep pool where dwelt a one-clawed lobster. It was hiding two yards under a rock, at the end of a cleft too narrow to swim up. Four times he tried to hook it out with his fore-pad, the claws of which were worn down with sand-scratching, and in his eagerness to get at it he tore seaweed with his teeth. The lobster had been disturbed many times in its life, for nearly every man of the villages of Cryde and Ham had tried to dislodge it with long sticks to which they had lashed hooks. The lobster had lost so many claws that, after nine had been wrenched off, its brain refused to grow any more. Its chief enemy was an old man named Muggy, who went to the pool every Sunday morning at low spring-tide with a rabbit-skin and entrails, which he threw into the water to lure it forth from the cleft. The lobster was too cunning, and so it lived.

The otters rested by day on a ledge in the cave under the headland. Here dwelt Jarrk the seal, who climbed a slab below them by shuffles and flapping jumps. Sometimes Tarka swam in the pools of the cave, rolling on his back to bite the drops of ironwater which dripped from the rocky roof, but only when Jarrk was away in the sea, hunting the conger where the rocks of Bag Leap ripped foam out of the tide.

The greatest conger of Bag Leap, who was Garbargee, had never been caught, for whenever it saw Jarrk the seal, its enemy, it hid far down in the crab-green water, in a hole in the rocks of the deepest pool, where lay shell-crusted cannon and gear of H.M. sloop *Weazel*, wrecked there a century before. When no seal was about, Garbargee hung out of the hole and stared, unblinkingly, for fish, which it pursued and swallowed. One morning as Tarka, hungry after a stormy night, was searching in the thong-weed five fathoms under the glimmering surface, something flashed above him, and looking up, he saw a narrow head with a long hooked preying beak and two large webs ready to thrust in chase of fish. This was Oylegrin the shag, whose oily greenish-black feathers reflected light. The smooth narrow head flickered as Oylegrin shifted his gaze, and a pollack below mistook the flicker for a smaller surface-swimming fish. The pollack turned to rise and take it, and the shag saw the gleam of its side at the same time as Tarka saw it. Oylegrin tipped up and kicked rapidly downwards faster than an otter could swim. His tight feathers glinted and gleamed as he pursued the pollack. Garbargee also saw the pollack and uncurled a muscular tail from its hold on a jut of rock. The conger was longer than a man is tall, and thicker through the body than Tarka. It weighed ninety pounds. It waved about the weedy timbers, and as it passed over, crabs hid in the mouths of cannon.

Bird, animal, and fish made a chasing arrow-head whose tip was the glinting pollack; conger the flexible shaft, otter and shag the barbs. Oylegrin swam with long neck stretched out, hooked beak ready to grip, while he thrust with webbed feet farther from the bubbles which ran out of his gullet. The pollack turned near Tarka, who swung up and followed it. Oylegrin braked and swerved with fourteen short stiff tail-feathers and one upturned web. The pollack turned down a sheer rock hung with thong-weed, but, meeting Tarka, turned up again and was caught by Oylegrin.

The chasing arrow-head buckled against the rock, in a tangle of thongs and ribbons and bubbles shaking up-wards. The giant conger had bitten the shag through the neck. Wings flapped, a grating, muffled cry broke out of a bottle of air. Tarka's mouth opened wide, but his teeth could not pierce the conger's skin. The gloom darkened, for an opaqueness was spreading where there had been movement.

Now Jarrk the seal, who had been searching round the base of the rock, saw an otter rising to the surface, and was swinging up towards him when he saw a conger eel wave out of the opaqueness, which was Oylegrin's blood staining the green gloom. Garbargee held the shag in its jaws. The undersea cloud was scattered by the swirls of flippers as the seal chased the conger. Garbargee dropped the shag, and the cleft of rock received its grey tenant. Jarrk swung up with a bend of his smooth body, and lay under the surface with only his head out, drinking fresh air, and looking at Tarka six yards away. *Wuff, wuff*, said Jarrk playfully. *Iss, iss* cried Tarka in alarm. The pollack escaped, and soon afterwards was feeding with other fish on the crab-nibbled corpse of the shag.

It was not often that the otters went fishing in daylight; usually they lay in the warm noonday sun on the sand of a cove behind the Long Rock—a spur of which was the plucking perch of Chakchek the One-eyed, the peregrine falcon. One morning Chakchek half-closed his wings and cut down at Tarka, crying *Aik-aik-aik!* and swishing past his head. It was the cream-breasted tiercel's cry of anger. He was a swift flyer and soon mounted to where his mate waited at her pitch in the sky above the precipice, scanning the lower airs for rock-dove, oyster-catcher, finch, or guillemot. When they had swept away down the north side of the landhead, Kronk the raven croaked thrice, deeply, and took the air to twirl with his mate in the windy up-trends.

Near Sandy Cove was the Cormorants' Rock, where five cormorants squatted during most of the daylit hours, digesting their cropfuls of fishes. Each cormorant, as it arrived with steady black flight, would pass the rock about fifty yards, swing round, and fly back into the wind, alighting uneasily among its brethren, some of whom had the tails of fishes sticking out of their gullets. They held out their wings and worked their shoulders to ease the fish down into their crops. The top of Cormorants' Rock, where they sat, was above the highest wave.

Bag Leap was a sunken reef stretching about half a mile from the point over which the tides raced. Here the currents brought many seals, which had followed salmon up the Severn Sea, on their return home to Lundy Island. With them was a grey seal, a stranger, who had come down from the north. For several days the seals fished off the Leap, while Jarrk roared among them and joined in their favourite game of chasing the smallest seal, who was not black and yellowish-brown like themselves, but a rare silvery-white. They would swim round the rocks looking for her, sometimes remaining under water for nearly a quarter of an hour. Once when Tarka was searching for a bass in four fathoms he met Jarrk face to face, and the shock made him blow a big bubble. He turned and kicked up to the light, while Jarrk swum round him in a spiral. Jarrk was always gentle, for he had never an enemy to shock him into fear, and when Tarka tissed and yikkered at him, the scimitar-shaped lip-bristles of his broad muzzle twitched, his upper lip lifted off his lower jaw, he showed his yellow teeth, and barked. *Wuff, wuff*, said Jarrk, jovially. *Ic-yang*, yikkered Tarka. The seal snorted; then his back, stretched and gleaming, rolled under like a barrel.

When the seals left Bag Leap for the seventeen-mile swim to their island home, one remained with Jarrk. She was the stranger grey seal, and often while the other seals had been romping, she had been exploring the far dark end of the cave behind the Long Rock, where was a beach of boulders. Greymuzzle explored the beach for the same purpose, and sometimes otter and seal passed by each other in the pools. On one high-tide the seal swam into the cave, and did not return with the ebb. For three days she hid herself, and then she flapped down the sand and splashed into the sea, very hungry.

Many times during the rise and fall of tides the bitch-otter ran into the cave, and on the morning of the grey seal's return to the sea she swam round the Long Rock and crawled out of the surge among the limpet-studded rocks of Bag Hole. Three hundred and ten feet above her, perched on the swarded lip of a sand-coloured cliff, Kronk the raven watched her running round and over boulders. She reached the base of the precipice, and scrambled up a slide of scree, which had clattered down during the rains of autumn. Gulls wove and interwove in flight below the raven, floating past their roosts in the face of the cliff. The scree had fallen from under the Wreckers' Path, made during centuries by the cautious feet of men and women descending after storms to gather what the sea had thrown on the boulders of the Hole. It was not much wider than one of the sheep-paths on the headland. Grey-muzzle ran along it, and turning a corner by a lichened boulder, disappeared from the sight of Kronk. She had climbed here alone several times during the previous night.

Less than a minute afterwards the raven jumped leisurely over the edge, and opening his wings, rose on the wind, and turning swept back over his perching place, over snares pegged by rabbit-runs in the grass, and to a shillet wall a hundred yards from the precipice. One of the brass snares Kronk was watching. It had been drawn tight about the neck of a rabbit since early morning; the rabbit had died after two hours of jumping and wheezing. It was cold; its fleas were swarming in agitation over its longer hairs. Kronk was waiting for a meal off the rabbit, but he did not like to go near it until he knew for certain that the trapper, whom he had watched setting the snare the afternoon before, had not tilled a gin beside it specially for Kronk. The raven knew all about the methods of trappers, and the gins and snares they tilled. Several times Kronk had sailed with the wind over the snared rabbit; he sailed without checking by tail or wing lest the trapper be spying upon him. In every other act of his life he was as cautious, having learned many things about man in more than a hundred years of flying.

The raven was waiting for Mewliboy, the cowardly soaring buzzard hawk, to espy the rabbit; and when Mewliboy had ripped it open with one stroke of his hooked beak, the raven intended to call *krok-krok-krok* rapidly, and so summon his mate to help him deal with the buzzard, if he were not trapped. And if he had sprung a hidden gin, then it would be safe for Kronk. So the raven reasoned.

Greymuzzle came to the end of Wreckers' Path, and climbed up springy clumps of sea-thrift, among gull-feathers and mussel-shells and fish-bones, and ran along another path to the top of the precipice. She looked left and right, often pausing to sniff the air. She picked up a feather, ran with it a few yards and dropped it again. She cast round over the sward, peering into rabbit-holes, and pulling out dry stalks of thrift that the wind had blown there. Kronk watched her running, swift and low, along the narrow, wandering lines pressed in the sward by the feet of rabbits; he saw her stop by the snared rabbit, bite on to its neck, and watched her tugging at it. *Crr-crr!* said Kronk to himself.

He jumped off the wall, which was covered with dry lichens dissolving the stones with acids, and circling above Greymuzzle, croaked a long, harsh note, meant to call the gulls. He dived at Greymuzzle, repeating the harsh cry, and very soon nearly fifty herring gulls were screaming about her. Alarmed by the noise, she ran back the way she had come; the gulls followed, and Kronk had the rabbit to himself. Seeing him, the gulls returned, screaming and flying as near to him as they dared. Kronk pecked and pulled at his ease, knowing that the gulls would give the alarm should a man come round either the south or the north side of the wall, which hid approach.

Greymuzzle was slipping down the scree at the end of Wreckers' Path, carrying a brown dry tussock of sea-thrift in her mouth, when the remote crying of gulls became loud above the cliff. *Quoc-quoc-quoac!* many were muttering in anger. Several hundred wheeled and floated above the otter. She heard a soughing of wings, and looking up saw the beak and eyes of the raven growing larger as he plunged towards her. He had taken nine long hops away from the rabbit, and the tenth had taken him over the precipice edge as a man, walking fast, had taken his ninth stride round the northern wall, three hundred yards off. Kronk opened his wings when half-way down the cliff and sailed without a wing-beat round the Point.

Mewing and scolding, the gulls floated higher in the wind, and hearing them, the grey seal, who had been lolling beyond the break of rollers, swam out twenty yards and turned to watch the top of the cliff. She knew that the tossing flight and the cries of *quoc-quoc-quoac!* meant the presence of man.

Greymuzzle swam round the Long Rock with the mat of roots in her mouth, and crawled out of the sandy surge. Tarka was lying on his back, playing with a smooth green flat pebble of glass that he had carried from the bed of a pool. When he saw her, he turned on his pads—neither bone nor muscle showed in action—and ran to see what she carried. Greymuzzle lifted her burden out of his playful way, but he jostled her, wanting to take it and knowing nothing of her purpose He bit off three rootlets, and at the mouth of the cave he ran back to his glass pebble.

The seal watched with bleary eyes the man climbing down, and his spaniel dog sitting three-quarters of the way down the path, frightened to follow its master farther. Tarka played with his pebble, hidden behind the orange-lichened and towering wall of the Long Rock. In a scattered and unled flock the gulls drifted above the cliff. Over them Kronk the raven, most powerful and black, cleaved the air on outspread wings; sometimes he twirled on his back, recovering immediately. He was practising the upward or impaling lunge of beak that he had learned from his father a hundred and thirteen years before. High above the raven a small dark star twinkled and swept in its orbit, twinkled and poised on its pitch. Chakchek the One-eyed, slate-blue-pinioned and cream-breasted, was aloft. *Crr-crr*, said Kronk, as sea and greensward turned up and over and upright again. *Crr-crr-crr*, as the man disappeared round the Long Rock, and Kronk sailed downwind to be over him.

A thousand feet below the raven, Tarka tapped his pebble of glass, green and dim as the light seen through the hollow waves rearing for their fall on the sand. The noise of waves, continuous and roaring on the rocks at low tide, was swelled by the echo beaten back by the cliff, and Tarka saw the man climbing round the Long Rock before he heard him. The man, jumping from boulder to boulder, did not see Tarka; but when he reached the sand he saw the trails of two otters. One trail led into the cave straitly, with regular five-toed prints, except where the track swerved from the impetuous and uneven trail of a galloping otter. Three rootlets of sea-thrift were dropped on the spurred sand. The strait trail led on; the other turned back to the wetted grey pebble, where lay crab-shells, corks, fishtails, and a piece of glass.

The man followed the strait tracks into the cave, into twilight, clambering over ice-cold rocks, and shining a light on the pools wherein drops glistened and struck loud in the stillness. He moved slowly, with glances over his shoulder at the diminishing circle of daylight. The roof of the cave was red and brown with the iron in the rock. Sometimes his foothold wobbled on a stone that in the motion of tides had worn a cup for itself. A hundred yards from its mouth the cave turned to the left, shutting dark-ness and sea-whispers together. The man went on, bend-ing down to find his way by the light he carried. The pools became shallower, without life or weed; the roof lower and dry. A wailing cry ran along the walls. Hold-ing the electric torch before him, he saw four pricks of light that moved, vanished, and appeared again, one pair above the other. The wail went past him again, like the cry of a hungry infant. On the grey boulder at his feet the wan light showed a black mark, as of tar on bitten fish-bones—the spraints of an otter.

In five minutes he had walked another fifty yards into the cave. The pale-yellow eyes shifted noiselessly in front of him. The toe of his boot kicked something that clattered on the stones, and looking down, he saw a bone; and near it, other bones, skulls, and shrunken hides. He picked up a jawbone, with grinder teeth, cuspless and oblique, set along it. Many seals had died in the cavern.

Again the wailing, not far away. The boulders sloped

upwards, and pressed one against another by his feet made a noise of pob-pobble that rang solidly and echoed down the cave and up again. Before them something white was stirring. Picking it up, he stroked the soft, warm hair of a baby seal, putting his finger in its mouth to stop the wailing. While he was nursing it, he heard the hollow echo of a plunging splash, a grumbling noise like *uch, uch!* and a slapping as of the palms of great hands on flat rocks. Turning his torch down into the gloom, he saw two dull red orbs, and heard the angry bleat of a mother seal.

He carried the white calf to the inner wall of the cave and laid it down; then hurried to the other wall, where ledges formed natural steps. On the top ledge an otter was crouching. By the shape of the head he knew it was a bitch-otter; an old otter, with grey and grizzled hairs on its muzzle. He climbed as high as he dared, and saw that it had made a couch of dry seaweed and grasses and thrift. He peered into the couch. The otter moved to and fro on the narrow ledge, tissing. He could see no cubs; nor did she appear to be in whelp.

Uch, uch! gasped the seal, exhausted and aching after her anguished journey over the boulders of the cavern. She had hurried by pressing the palms of her flippers on the ground and lifting her body forward by short jumps, moving fast as a walking man. She reached her cub and caressed it with her tongue, making sounds over it between sobbing and bleating. Then she turned her back to the man, and flung sand and pebbles at him with quick scooping strokes of her flippers. The man took from his pocket a wooden whistle made from an elderberry stick and played several soft tunes upon it. The seal looked at him, enjoying the rude music. She lay still and happy with her calf, whose head was turned on one side as it sucked through the side of its mouth. The man played on, moving nearer to the seal. Slowly he bent down to stroke its head, and the seal licked his hand.

5 *Adolf*

D. H. LAWRENCE

WHEN WE were children our father often worked
on the night shift. Once it was springtime, and
he used to arrive home, black and tired, just
as we were downstairs in our night-dresses. Then night
met morning face to face, and the contact was not always
happy. Perhaps it was painful to my father to see us gaily
entering upon the day into which he dragged himself
soiled and weary. He didn't like going to bed in the spring
morning sunshine.

But sometimes he was happy, because of his long walk
through the dewy fields in the first daybreak. He loved
the open morning, the crystal and the space, after a night
down pit. He watched every bird, every stir in the
trembling grass, answered the whinnying of the pewits
and tweeted to the wrens. If he could, he also would have
whinnied and tweeted and whistled in a native language
that was not human. He liked non-human things best.

One sunny morning we were all sitting at table when
we heard his heavy slurring walk up the entry. We
became uneasy. His was always a disturbing presence,
trammelling. He passed the window darkly, and we heard
him go into the scullery and put down his tin bottle. But
directly he came into the kitchen. We felt at once that he
had something to communicate. No one spoke. We
watched his black face for a second.

"Give me a drink," he said.

My mother hastily poured out his tea. He went to pour it out into his saucer. But instead of drinking he suddenly put something on the table among the teacups. A tiny brown rabbit! A small rabbit, a mere morsel, sitting against the bread as still as if it were a made thing.

"A rabbit! A young one! Who gave it you, Father?"

But he laughed enigmatically, with a sliding motion of his yellow-grey eyes, and went to take off his coat. We pounced on the rabbit.

"Is it alive? Can you feel its heart beat?"

My father came back and sat down heavily in his armchair. He dragged his saucer to him, and blew his tea, pushing out his red lips under his black moustache.

"Where did you get it, Father?"

"I picked it up," he said, wiping his naked forearm over his mouth and beard.

"Where?"

"It is a wild one!" came my mother's quick voice.

"Yes, it is."

"Then why did you bring it?" cried my mother.

"Oh, we wanted it," came our cry.

"Yes, I've no doubt you did——" retorted my mother. But she was drowned in our clamour of questions.

On the field path my father had found a dead mother rabbit and three dead little ones—this one alive, but unmoving.

"But what had killed them, Daddy?"

"I couldn't say, my child. I s'd think she'd aten something."

"Why did you bring it!" again my mother's voice of condemnation. "You know what it will be."

My father made no answer, but we were loud in protest.

"He must bring it. It's not big enough to live by itself. It would die," we shouted.

"Yes, and it will die now. And then there'll be *another* outcry."

My mother set her face against the tragedy of dead pets. Our hearts sank.

"It won't die, Father, will it? Why will it? It won't."

"I s'd think not," said my father.

"You know well enough it will. Haven't we had it all before!" said my mother.

"They dunna always pine," replied my father testily.

But my mother reminded him of other little wild animals he had brought, which had sulked and refused to live, and brought storms of tears and trouble in our house of lunatics.

Trouble fell on us. The little rabbit sat on our lap, unmoving, its eye wide and dark. We brought it milk, warm milk, and held it to its nose. It sat as still as if it was far away, retreated down some deep burrow, hidden, oblivious. We wetted its mouth and whiskers with drops of milk. It gave no sign, did not even shake off the wet white drops. Somebody began to shed a few secret tears.

"What did I say?" cried my mother. "Take it and put it down in the field."

Her command was in vain. We were driven to get dressed for school. There sat the rabbit. It was like a tiny obscure cloud. Watching it, the emotions died out of our breast. Useless to love it, to yearn over it. Its little feelings were all ambushed. They must be circumvented. Love and affection were a trespass upon it. A little wild thing, it became more mute and asphyxiated still in its own arrest, when we approached with love. We must not love it. We must circumvent it, for its own existence.

So I passed the order to my sister and my mother. The rabbit was not to be spoken to, nor even looked at. Wrapping it in a piece of flannel, I put it in an obscure corner of the cold parlour, and put a saucer of milk before its nose. My mother was forbidden to enter the parlour while we were at school.

"As if I should take any notice of your nonsense," she cried, affronted. Yet I doubt if she ventured into the parlour.

At midday, after school, creeping into the front room, there we saw the rabbit still and unmoving in the piece of flannel. Strange grey-brown neutralization of life, still living! It was a sore problem to us.

"Why won't it drink its milk, Mother?" we whispered. Our father was asleep.

"It prefers to sulk its life away, silly little thing." A profound problem. Prefers to sulk its life away! We put young dandelion leaves to its nose. The sphinx was not more oblivious. Yet its eye was bright.

At tea-time, however, it had hopped a few inches, out of its flannel, and there it sat again, uncovered, a little solid cloud of muteness, brown, with unmoving whiskers. Only its side palpitated slightly with life.

Darkness came; my father set off to work. The rabbit was still unmoving. Dumb despair was coming over the sisters, a threat of tears before bedtime. Clouds of my mother's anger gathered as she muttered against my father's wantonness.

Once more the rabbit was wrapped in the old pit singlet. But now it was carried into the scullery and put under the copper fire-place, that it might imagine itself inside a burrow. The saucers were placed about, four or five, here and there on the floor, so that if the little creature *should* chance to hop abroad, it could not fail to come upon some food. After this my mother was allowed to take from the scullery what she wanted and then she was forbidden to open the door.

When morning came and it was light, I went downstairs. Opening the scullery door, I heard a slight scuffle. Then I saw dabbles of milk all over the floor and tiny rabbit-droppings in the saucers. And there was the miscreant, the tips of his ears showing behind a pair of boots. I peeped at him. He sat bright-eyed and askance, twitching his nose and looking at me while not looking at me.

He was alive—very much alive. But still we were afraid to trespass much on his confidence.

"Father!" My father was arrested at the door. "Father the rabbit's alive."

"Back your life it is," said my father.

"Mind how you go in."

By evening, however, the little creature was tame, quite tame. He was christened Adolf. We were enchanted by him. We couldn't really love him, because he was wild and loveless to the end. But he was an unmixed delight.

We decided he was too small to live in a hutch—he

must live at large in the house. My mother protested, but in vain. He was so tiny. So we had him upstairs, and he dropped his tiny pills on the bed and we were enchanted.

Adolf made himself instantly at home. He had the run of the house, and was perfectly happy, with his tunnels and his holes behind the furniture.

We loved him to take meals with us. He would sit on the table humping his back, sipping his milk, shaking his whiskers and his tender ears, hopping off and hobbling back to his saucer, with an air of supreme unconcern. Suddenly he was alert. He hobbled a few tiny paces, and reared himself up inquisitively at the sugar basin. He fluttered his tiny fore-paws, and then reached and laid them on the edge of the basin, while he craned his thin neck and peeped in. He trembled his whiskers at the sugar, then did his best to lift down a lump.

"*Do* you think I will have it! Animals in the sugar pot!" cried my mother, with a rap of her hand on the table.

Which so delighted the electric Adolf that he flung his hindquarters and knocked over a cup.

"It's your own fault, Mother. If you left him alone——"

He continued to take tea with us. He rather liked warm tea. And he loved sugar. Having nibbled a lump, he would turn to the butter. There he was shooed off by our parent. He soon learned to treat her shooing with indifference. Still, she hated him to put his nose in the food. And he loved to do it. And one day between them they overturned the cream-jug. Adolf deluged his little chest, bounced back in terror, was seized by his little ears by my mother and bounced down on the hearth-rug. There he shivered in momentary discomfort, and suddenly set off in a wild flight to the parlour.

This last was his happy hunting-ground. He had cultivated the bad habit of pensively nibbling certain bits of cloth in the hearth-rug. When chased from this pasture he would retreat under the sofa. There he would twinkle in Buddhist meditation until suddenly, no one knew why he would go off like an alarm clock. With a sudden bumping scuffle he would whirl out of the room, going through the doorway with his little ears flying. Then we would hear his thunderbolt hurtling in the parlour, but before we could follow, the wild streak of Adolf would flash past us, on an electric wind that swept him round the scullery and carried him back, a little mad thing, flying possessed like a ball round the parlour. After which ebullition he would sit in a corner composed and distant, twitching his whiskers in abstract meditation. And it was in vain we questioned him about his outbursts. He just went off like a gun, and was as calm after it as a gun that smokes placidly.

Alas, he grew up rapidly. It was almost impossible to keep him from the outer door.

One day, as we were playing by the stile, I saw his brown shadow loiter across the road and pass into the field that faced the houses. Instantly a cry of "Adolf!"—a cry he knew full well. And instantly a wind swept him away down the sloping meadow, his tail twinkling and zigzagging through the grass. After him we pelted. It was a strange sight to see him, ears back, his little loins so powerful, flinging the world behind him. We ran ourselves out of breath, but could not catch him. Then somebody headed him off, and he sat with sudden unconcern, twitching his nose under a bunch of nettles.

His wanderings cost him a shock. One Sunday morning my father had just been quarrelling with a pedlar and we were hearing the aftermath indoors, when there came a sudden unearthly scream from the yard. We flew out. There sat Adolf cowering under a bench, while a great black-and-white cat glowered intently at him, a few yards away. Sight not to be forgotten. Adolf rolling back his eyes and parting his strange muzzle in another scream, the cat stretching forward in a slow elongation.

Ha, how we hated that cat! How we pursued him over the chapel wall and across the neighbours' gardens!

Adolf was still only half grown.

"Cats!" said my mother. "Hideous detestable animals, why do people harbour them?"

But Adolf was becoming too much for her. He dropped too many pills. And suddenly to hear him clumping downstairs when she was alone in the house was startling. And to keep him from the door was impossible. Cats prowled outside. It was worse than having a child to look after.

Yet we would not have him shut up. He became more lusty, more callous than ever. He was a strong kicker, and many a scratch on face and arms did we owe to him. But he brought his own doom on himself. The lace curtains in the parlour—my mother was rather proud of them—fell on the floor very full. One of Adolf's joys was to scuffle wildly through them as though through some foamy undergrowth. He had already torn rents in them.

One day he entangled himself altogether. He kicked,

he whirled round in a mad, nebulous inferno. He screamed—and brought down the curtain-rod with a smash, right on the best-beloved pelargonium, just as my mother rushed in. She extricated him, but she never forgave him. And he never forgave either. A heartless wildness had come over him.

Even we understood that he must go. It was decided, after a long deliberation, that my father should carry him back to the wildwoods. Once again he was stowed into the great pocket of the pit jacket.

"Best pop him i' th' pot," said my father, who enjoyed raising the wind of indignation.

And so, next day, our father said that Adolf, set down on the edge of the coppice, had hopped away with utmost indifference, neither elated nor moved. We heard it and believed. But many, many were the heart-searchings. How would the other rabbits receive him? Would they smell his tameness, his humanized degradation, and rend him? My mother pooh-poohed the extravagant idea.

However, he was gone, and we were rather relieved. My father kept an eye open for him. He declared that several times passing the coppice in the early morning, he had seen Adolf peeping through the nettle-stalks. He had called him, in an odd, high-voiced, cajoling fashion. But Adolf had not responded. Wildness gains so soon upon its creatures. And they become so contemptuous then of our tame presence. So it seemed to me. I myself would go to the edge of the coppice, and call softly. I myself would imagine bright eyes between the nettle-stalks, flash of a white, scornful tail past the bracken. That insolent white tail, as Adolf turned his flank on us!

6 *The Great Bear*

CHARLES READE

O NE DAY, being in a forest a few leagues from
Düsseldorf, as Gerard was walking like one in a
dream, his companion laid a hand on his shoulder,
and strung his crossbow with glittering eye. "Hush!" said
he, in a low whisper that startled Gerard more than
thunder. Gerard grasped his axe tight, and shook a little:
he heard a rustling in the wood hard by, and at the same
moment Denys sprang into the wood, and his crossbow
went to his shoulder, even as he jumped. Twang! went
the metal string; and after an instant's suspense he roared,
"Run forward, guard the road, he is hit! he is hit!"

Gerard darted forward, and as he ran a young bear burst out of the wood right upon him; finding itself intercepted, it went upon its hind legs with a snarl, and though not half grown, opened formidable jaws and long claws. Gerard, in a fury of excitement and agitation, flung himself on it, and delivered a tremendous blow on its nose with his axe, and the creature staggered; another, and it lay grovelling, with Gerard hacking it.

"Hallo! stop! you are mad to spoil the meat."

"I took it for a robber," said Gerard, panting. "I mean, I had made ready for a robber, so I could not hold my hand."

"Ay, these chattering travellers have stuffed your head full of thieves and assassins; they have not got a real live robber in their whole nation. Nay, I'll carry the beast; bear thou my crossbow."

"We will carry it by turns, then," said Gerard, "for 'tis a heavy load: poor thing, how its blood drips. Why did we slay it?"

"For supper, and the reward the baillie of the next town shall give us."

"And for that it must die, when it had but just begun to live; and perchance it hath a mother that will miss it sore this night, and loves it as ours love us; more than mine does me."

"What, know you not that his mother was caught in a pitfall last month, and her skin is now at the tanner's? and his father was stuck full of clothyard shafts t'other day, and died like Julius Caesar, with his hands folded on his bosom, and a dead dog in each of them?"

But Gerard would not view it jestingly. "Why, then,"

said he, "we have killed one of God's creatures that was all alone in the world—as I am this day, in this strange land."

"You young milksop," roared Denys, "these things must not be looked at so, or not another bow would be drawn nor quarrel fly in forest nor battlefield. Why, one of your kidney consorting with a troop of pikemen should turn them to a row of milk-pails; it is ended, to Rome thou goest not alone, for never wouldst thou reach the Alps in a whole skin. Some honest Burgundian shall go with thee as far as Lyons; and much I doubt that honest fellow will be myself, into whose liquor thou has dropped sundry powders to make me love thee; for erst I endured not doves in doublet and hose. From Lyons, I say, I can trust thee by ship to Italy, which being by all accounts the very stronghold of milksops, thou wilt there be safe; they will hear thy words, and make thee their duke in a twinkling."

Gerard sighed. "In sooth I love not to think of this Düsseldorf, where we are to part company, good friend."

They walked silently, each thinking of the separation at hand; the thought checked trifling conversation, and at these moments it is a relief to do something, however insignificant. Gerard asked Denys to lend him a bolt. "I have often shot with a long bow, but never with one of these!"

"Draw thy knife and cut this one out of the cub," said Denys slyly.

"Nay, nay, I want a clean one."

Denys gave him three out of his quiver.

Gerard strung the bow, and levelled it at a bough that had fallen into the road at some distance. The power of the instrument surprised him; the short but thick steel bow jarred him to the very heel as it went off, and the swift steel shaft was invisible in its passage; only the dead leaves, with which November had carpeted the narrow road, flew about on the other side of the bough.

"Ye aimed a thought too high," said Denys.

Gerard did not answer, for his ear was attracted by a sound behind them. It was a peculiar sound, too, like something heavy, but not hard, rushing softly over the dead leaves. He turned round with some little curiosity. A colossal creature was coming down the road at about sixty paces' distance.

He looked at it in a sort of calm stupor at first, but the next moment he turned ashy pale.

"Denys!" he cried. "Oh, God! Denys!"

Denys whirled round.

It was a bear as big as a cart-horse.

It was tearing along with its huge head down, running on a hot scent.

The very moment he saw it Denys said in a sickening whisper:

"The cub!"

Oh! the concentrated horror of that one word, whispered hoarsely, with dilating eyes! For in that syllable it all flashed upon them both like a sudden stroke of lightning in the dark—the bloody trail, the murdered cub, the mother upon them, *and it*. Death.

All this in a moment of time. The next, she saw them. Huge as she was, she seemed to double herself (it was her long hair bristling with rage): she raised her head big as a bull's, her swine-shaped jaws opened wide at them, her eyes turned to blood and flame, and she rushed upon them, scattering the leaves about her like a whirlwind as she came.

"Shoot!" screamed Denys, but Gerard stood shaking from head to foot, useless.

"Shoot, man! ten thousand devils, shoot! too late! Tree! tree!" and he dropped the cub, pushed Gerard across the road, and flew to the first tree and climbed it, Gerard the same on his side; and as they fled, both men uttered inhuman howls like savage creatures grazed by death.

With all their speed one or other would have been torn to fragments at the foot of his tree; but the bear stopped a moment at the cub.

Without taking her bloodshot eyes off those she was hunting, she smelt it all round, and found, how, her Creator only knows, that it was dead, quite dead. She gave a yell such as neither of the hunted ones had ever heard, nor dreamed to be in nature, and flew after Denys. She reared and struck at him as he climbed. He was just out of reach.

Instantly she seized the tree, and with her huge teeth tore a great piece out of it with a crash. Then she reared again, dug her claws deep into the bark, and began to mount it slowly, but as surely as a monkey.

Denys' evil star had led him to a dead tree, a mere shaft, and of no very great height. He climbed faster than his pursuer, and was soon at the top. He looked this way and that for some bough of another tree to spring to. There was none; and if he jumped down he knew the bear would be upon him ere he could recover the fall, and make short work of him. Moreover, Denys was little used to turning his back on danger, and his blood was rising at being hunted. He turned to bay.

"My hour is come," thought he. "Let me meet death like a man." He kneeled down and grasped a small shoot to steady himself, drew his long knife, and clenching his teeth, prepared to jab the huge brute as soon as it should mount within reach.

Of this combat the result was not doubtful.

The monster's head and neck were scarce vulnerable for bone and masses of hair. The man was going to sting the bear, and the bear to crack the man like a nut.

Gerard's heart was better than his nerves. He saw his friend's mortal danger, and passed at once from fear to blindish rage. He slipped down his tree in a moment, caught up the crossbow, which he had dropped in the road, and running furiously up, sent a bolt into the bear's body with a loud shout. The bear gave a snarl of rage and pain, and turned its head irresolutely.

"Keep aloof!" cried Denys, "or you are a dead man."

"I care not;" and in a moment he had another bolt ready and shot it fiercely into the bear, screaming, "Take that! take that!"

Denys poured a volley of oaths down at him. "Get away, idiot!"

He was right: the bear, finding so formidable and noisy a foe behind her, slipped growling down the tree, rending deep furrows in it as she slipped. Gerard ran back to his tree and climbed it swiftly. But while his legs were dangling some eight feet from the ground, the bear came rearing and struck with her fore paw, and out flew a piece of bloody cloth from Gerard's hose. He climbed and climbed; and presently he heard as it were in the air a voice say, "Go out on the bough!" He looked, and there was a long massive branch before him shooting upwards at a slight angle: he threw his body across it, and by a series of convulsive efforts worked up it to the end.

Then he looked round panting.

The bear was mounting the tree on the other side. He heard her claws scrape, and saw her bulge on both sides of the massive tree. Her eye not being very quick, she reached the fork and passed it, mounting the main stem. Gerard drew breath more freely. The bear either heard him or found by scent she was wrong; she paused; presently she caught sight of him. She eyed him steadily, then quietly descended to the fork.

Slowly and cautiously she stretched out a paw and tried the bough. It was a stiff oak branch, sound as iron. Instinct taught the creature this: it crawled carefully out on the bough, growling savagely as it came.

Gerard looked wildly down. He was forty feet from the ground. Death below. Death moving slow but sure on him in a still more horrible form. His hair bristled. The sweat poured from him. He sat helpless, fascinated, tongue-tied.

The bear crawled on. And now the stupor of death fell on the doomed man; he saw the open jaws and blood-shot eyes coming, but in a mist.

As in a mist he heard a twang; he glanced down; Denys, white and silent, was shooting up at the bear. The bear snarled at the twang, but crawled on. Again the crossbow twanged, and the bear snarled, and came nearer. Again the crossbow twanged; and the next moment the bear was close upon Gerard, where he sat, with hair standing stiff on end and eyes starting from their sockets, palsied. The bear opened her jaws like a grave, and hot blood spouted from them upon Gerard as from a pump. The bough rocked. The wounded monster was reeling; it clung, it stuck its sickles of claws deep into the wood; it toppled, its claws held firm, but its body rolled off, and the sudden shock to the branch shook Gerard forward on his stomach with his face upon one of the bear's straining paws. At this, by a convulsive effort, she raised her head up, up, till he felt her hot fetid breath. Then huge teeth snapped together loudly close below him in the air, with a last effort of baffled hate. The ponderous carcass rent the claws out of the bough, then pounded the earth with a tremendous thump. There was a shout of triumph below, and the very next instant a cry of dismay, for Gerard had swooned, and without an attempt to save himself rolled headlong from the perilous height.

7 *Python up a Tree*

DAVID ATTENBOROUGH

A
FTER THE initial declaration of our interest in
animals, I feared the villagers were disappointed
that Charles Lagus and I had not produced rifles
and begun hunting tigers. They were certainly mystified
when they found that we spent our days observing such
common and undramatic creatures as ants and little
lizards. Our friend the old man, however, did not lose
faith. Every day he came to see us. Sometimes he brought
a small lizard or a centipede with him. Once he produced
a bowl full of puffer fish, each furiously inflating itself
into a creamy-coloured ball. Two days before we were

due to leave the village, he marched jubilantly up to our hut at the head of a small delegation.

"*Selamat pagi*," I said. "Peace on the morning."

In reply, he pushed forward a young boy who spoke to us in Malay. Laboriously we discovered that the lad had been gathering rattan cane in the forest the day before when he had seen an enormous snake.

"*Besar*," said the boy. "Big. Big."

To demonstrate the dimensions of this monster, he drew a line with his toe in the dust of the floor, took six long paces away from it and drew another line. "*Besar*," he repeated, pointing from one line to the other.

We agreed.

There are only two snakes found in Java which attain such a size, and both are pythons. The Indian Python grows to a length of twenty-five feet and the Reticulate Python even longer, one monstrous example having been recorded as being thirty-two feet long, a measurement which qualified it as being the largest snake in the world. If the snake the boy had seen was indeed eighteen feet long it would be a formidable creature to tackle, for a man caught in its coils would almost certainly be squeezed to death. I recalled promising the London Zoo that if we could catch a "nice big python" we would do so.

The accepted method of capturing such monsters is simple and comparatively fool-proof. It requires a minimum of three men, and for preference the recipe recommends one man for each yard of snake. This body of eager and intrepid hunters should stand at a distance from the snake while the leader allocates duties. One man must be made responsible for the head, one for the tail, and the rest for the intervening coils. Then, on a word of command, every man leaps at the snake and grasps the section for which he is responsible. For complete success, it is important that at least the head-man and the tail-man should grab simultaneously, for if the snake has one free end it is able to wrap itself round the man dealing with the other end, and begin squeezing. It follows, therefore, that a vital ingredient of the recipe is complete mutual confidence between all members of the team.

I looked at the turbaned group in front of me with a certain amount of misgiving. I was not doubtful of their courage individually, but I was very unsure of my ability to convey to them, without any possibility of a misunderstanding, my plan of campaign.

I talked for a long time. I drew patterns in the dust. At the end of a quarter of an hour I had succeeded in explaining enough of my plan to convince five of the men that they would have no part of it. There remained the old man and the boy. Charles was duty-bound to be filming the operation. I proposed that the old man should leap for the tail, the boy for the middle, and I would be responsible for the head. It might seem from this that I was claiming the most hazardous task, but in fact it was the job I much preferred. Although I ran the risk of being bitten, a python's fangs are not poisonous and cannot inflict anything worse than a bad scratch. On the other hand, the man dealing with the tail is liable to have a rather more unpleasant time, for a snake when it is being attacked nearly always ejects from its rear a large quantity of particularly foul-smelling excreta.

As far as I could gather, both the old man and the boy

understood the plan and had agreed to help, so we gathered together our equipment and set off into the forest. The boy walked ahead cutting a path through the dense undergrowth with his *parang*. I walked behind him with a large sack and a rope. Behind me came the old man carrying some of the photographic equipment, and Charles brought up the rear with his camera ready loaded in his hand. It would be untruthful to pretend that I was not a little nervous. Although I have an intense dislike of handling poisonous snakes, where one miscalculation can mean weeks of extreme agony and possibly death, I have a considerable affection for the non-poisonous pythons and boas. But I had never tackled one larger than four feet long, and I was not overwhelmingly confident that the men who were to help me had anything but the dimmest idea of what I expected them to do when my plan went into operation and I shouted, "*Mendja-lankan*." I had culled this word from my dictionary, which assured me that it meant "make go: execute"; I devoutly hoped that it was right.

Soon the ground steepened. We climbed past clumps of bamboo. Black dust and brittle fragments of dry leaves showered down on us and stuck to our sweating bodies as we forced our way between the creaking stems. As we passed through a clearing I had a sudden glimpse over the crowns of the trees growing on the slope below us and across the broad sweep of the bay to the kampong, a mile away. The boy ahead stopped and pointed to the ground. Rusting tags of iron wire and the sharp corner of a broken concrete block projected incongruously from beneath a carpet of leafy creepers. We stepped over it and found beyond a deep concrete-lined pit almost entirely concealed beneath the vegetation. Near by a trench contoured the hill. I was reminded of pictures of the ancient monuments of Central America and Indo-China which were discovered deserted and overwhelmed by the forest.

The boy spoke.

"Boom! Boom!" he said. "*Besar. Orang Djepang.*"

We had stumbled upon the remains of a gun emplacement built only thirteen years earlier by the Japanese when they had invaded and occupied the whole of Java.

We walked onwards, higher up the side of the hill. At last the boy stopped. He had seen the snake near here, he said. We dumped our equipment and each of us took a different path through the bush, searching for the creature. It seemed a hopeless task. As I looked up into the maze of lianas entangling the branches of the trees, I doubted whether I should have seen the snake even if it had been in front of my eyes. Suddenly I heard the old man calling excitedly. As quickly as I could, I rushed to him. He was standing at the foot of a small tree in a clearing. As I reached him he pointed into the branches above. Looped over one of the boughs I saw the glistening flank of a giant snake. But this was all I could see; among the confusing dapples of light and shade, of luxuriant leaves and interlacing creepers, I could not distinguish either its head or its tail. This was inconvenient; my snake-catching recipe made no mention of how to deal with giant snakes when they were in trees. I was quite certain, however, that the snake would be a better climber than I, and it was no part of my plan to have a wrestling match with one in a tree. The only solution was to get it out of the tree and on to the ground so that we could put our carefully arranged plan into action. With my *parang* in my hand, I swung myself up into the tree. The branch around which the snake had draped itself was about thirty feet above the ground. As I approached it, I saw to my relief that the reptile was lying at least ten feet along it, away from the trunk. Its flat triangular head rested on one of its enormous coils, looking straight at me with its yellow button-like eyes. It was a beautiful creature, its smooth polished body richly patterned in black, brown, and yellow. It was difficult to judge its length, but the largest coil I could see was at least a foot in girth. I braced my back against the trunk behind me and with hurried blows of my *parang* began cutting through the base of the branch.

The monster continued staring at me with a steadfast unblinking gaze. As the branch shook beneath my *parang* the reptile lifted its head, hissed, and flickered its long black tongue. One of its coils began slithering smoothly over the branch. I redoubled my efforts. The bough creaked and slowly hinged downwards. With two more blows it fell clear, carrying the python with it, and landed with a crash close by the boy and the old man.

"*Mendjalankan!*" I roared. "Make go: execute!"

They gaped at me uncomprehendingly.

I saw the snake's head appear from between the leaves of the fallen branch and it began sliding out, heading for a clump of bamboo on the other side of the clearing. If it reached this and succeeded in entwining itself among the massive bases of the bamboo stems we should never catch it.

I began scrambling down the tree as fast as I could. *"Mendjalankan!"* I bawled in exasperation at my team, who were standing beside Charles and his camera, watching dumbfounded.

With a final jump I landed on the ground, seized the sack, and ran after the snake, which was now within three yards of the bamboo. If we were going to catch it I should have to tackle it myself. Fortunately it was so intent on reaching the bamboo that it paid no regard whatsoever to me as I ran after it, but continued wriggling onwards with surprising rapidity for so large a snake.

I caught up with it just before its head entered the bamboo. I snatched its tail and jerked it backwards. Infuriated by this indignity, it turned on me, opened its mouth, and drew its head back in a striking position, its black tongue flickering in and out. I took the sack in my right hand and threw it, like a fisherman casting a net, so that it dropped neatly over its head.

"Hoop-la!" yelled Charles from behind his camera.

I pounced on the sack, and fumbling in the folds, gripped the snake by the scruff of its neck. Then quickly, remembering the recipe, I grabbed its tail with my other hand. I stood up in triumph. The great snake twisted and struggled, coiling itself into loops. Its body, which I estimated was at least twelve feet long, was so heavy and cumbersome that though I raised its head and tail above my head its middle coils still lay on the ground.

It was at this moment, as I held the snake aloft, that the boy at last decided to come to my assistance. He arrived just in time to receive a jet of foul fluid all over his sarong. The old man sat down and laughed until tears ran down his cheeks.

8 *The Thak Man-eater*

JIM CORBETT

AFTER BREAKFAST I took one of the buffaloes and set out for Thak, intending to tie it up on the spot where the man had been killed. The Headman had given me a very graphic account of the events of that date, for he himself had nearly fallen a victim to the tigress. It appeared that towards the afternoon, accompanied by his granddaughter, a girl ten years of age, he had gone to dig up ginger tubers in a field some sixty yards from his house. This field is about half an acre in extent and is surrounded on three sides by jungle, and being on the slope of a fairly steep hill it is visible from the Headman's house. After the old man and his granddaughter had been at work for some time, his wife, who was husking rice in the courtyard of the house, called out in a very agitated voice and asked him if he was deaf that he could not hear the pheasants and other birds that were chattering in the jungle above him. Fortunately for him, he acted promptly. Dropping his hoe, he grabbed the child's hand, and together they ran back to the house, urged on by the woman, who said she could now see a red animal in the bushes at the upper end of the field. Half an hour later the tigress killed a man who was lopping branches off a tree in a field three hundred yards from the Headman's house.

It was a small gnarled tree growing out of a three-foot-high bank between two terraced fields, and had been lopped year after year for cattle fodder. The man who had been killed was standing on the trunk holding one branch and cutting another when the tigress came up from behind, tore his hold from the branch, and, after killing him, carried him away into the dense brush-wood bordering the fields.

Like all other villages in Kumaon, Thak during its hundreds of years of existence has passed through many vicissitudes, but never before in its long history had it been deserted as it now was. On my previous visits I had found it a hive of industry, but when I went up to it on this afternoon, taking the young buffalo with me, silence reigned over it. Every one of the hundred or more inhabitants had fled, taking their livestock with them—the only animal I saw in the village was a cat, which gave me a warm welcome; so hurried had the evacuation been that many of the doors of the houses had been left wide open. On every path in the village, in the courtyard of the houses, and in the dust before all the doors I found the tigress's pug marks. The open doorways were a menace, for the path as it wound through the village passed close to them, and in any of the houses the tigress may have been lurking.

From the terraced fields above the cattle shelters a bird's-eye view of the village is obtained, and it was not difficult, from the description the Headman had given me, to locate the tree where the tigress had secured her last victim. In the soft earth under the tree there were signs of a struggle and a few clots of dried blood. From here the tigress had carried her kill a hundred yards over a ploughed field, through a stout hedge, and into the dense brushwood beyond. The footprints from the village and back the way they had come showed that the entire population of the village had visited the scene of the kill, but from the tree to the hedge there was only one track, the track the tigress had made when carrying away her victim. No attempt had been made to follow her up and recover the body.

Scraping away a little earth from under the tree I exposed a root, and to this root I tied my buffalo, bedding it down with a liberal supply of hay taken from a nearby stack.

The village, which is on the north face of the hill, was now in shadow, and if I was to get back to camp before dark it was time for me to make a start. Skirting round the village to avoid the menace of the open doorways, I joined the path below the houses.

This path after it leaves the village passes under a giant mango tree, from the roots of which issues a cold spring of clear water. After running along a groove cut in a massive slab of rock, this water falls into a rough masonry trough, from where it spreads on to the surrounding ground, rendering it soft and slushy. I had drunk at the spring on my way up, leaving my footprints in this slushy ground, and on approaching the spring now for a second drink, I found the tigress's pug marks superimposed on my footprints. After quenching her thirst the tigress had avoided the path and had gained the village by climbing a steep bank overgrown with strobilanthes and nettles, and taking up a position in the shelter of one of the houses, had possibly watched me while I was tying up the buffalo, expecting me to return the way I had gone; it was fortunate for me that I had noted the danger of passing those open doorways a second time, and had taken the longer way round.

Breakfast disposed of on the morning of the 25th, I took a second buffalo and set out for Thak. The path, after leaving the cultivated land at Chuka, skirts along the foot of the hill for about half a mile before it divides. One arm goes straight up a ridge to Thak and the other, after continuing along the foot of the hill for another half-mile, zigzags up through Kumaya Chak to Kot Kindri.

At the divide I found the pug marks of the tigress and followed them all the way back to Thak. The fact that she had come down the hill after me the previous evening was proof that she had not killed the buffalo. This, though very disappointing, was not at all unusual, for tigers will on occasions visit an animal that is tied up for several nights in succession before they finally kill it, for tigers do not kill unless they are hungry.

Leaving the second buffalo at the mango tree, where there was an abundance of green grass, I skirted round the houses and found No. 1 buffalo sleeping peacefully after a big feed and a disturbed night. The tigress, coming from the direction of the village as her pug marks showed, had approached to within a few feet of the buffalo, and had then gone back the way she had come. Taking the buffalo down to the spring, I let it graze for an hour or two, and then took it back and tied it up at the same spot where it had been the previous night.

As in three days I had seen the man-eater's tracks five times on the path leading to Thak, I decided to sit up over the path and try to get a shot at her that way. To give me warning of the tigress's approach I tied a goat with a bell round its neck on the path, and at 4 p.m. I climbed into the tree. I told my men to return at 8 a.m. the following morning, and began my watch.

At sunset a cold wind started blowing, and while I was attempting to pull a coat over my shoulders the ropes on one side of the machan slipped, rendering my seat very uncomfortable. An hour later a storm came on, and though it did not rain for long it wet me to the skin, greatly adding to my discomfort. During the sixteen hours I sat in the tree I did not see or hear anything. The men turned up at 8 a.m. I returned to camp for a hot bath and a good meal, and then, accompanied by six of my men, set out for Thak.

The overnight rain had washed all the old tracks off the path, and two hundred yards above the tree I had sat in

I found the fresh pug marks of the tigress, where she had come out of the jungle and gone up the path in the direction of Thak. Very cautiously I stalked the first buffalo, only to find it lying asleep on the path; the tigress had skirted round it, rejoined the path a few yards farther on, and continued up the hill. Following on her tracks, I approached the second buffalo, and as I got near the place where it had been tied two blue Himalayan magpies rose off the ground and went screaming down the hill.

The presence of these birds indicated (a) that the buffalo was dead, (b) that it had been partly eaten and not carried away, and (c) that the tigress was not in the close vicinity.

On arrival at the stump to which it had been tied I saw that the buffalo had been dragged off the path and partly eaten, and on examining the animal I found it had not been killed by the tigress but that it had in all probability died of snake-bite (there were many hamadryads in the surrounding jungles), and that, finding it lying dead on the path, the tigress had eaten a meal off it and had then tried to drag it away. When she found she could not break the rope she had partly covered it over with dry leaves and brushwood and continued on her way up to Thak.

On my way up from Chuka I had dismantled the machan I had sat on the previous night, and while two of my men climbed into the almond tree to make a seat for me—the tree was not big enough for a machan—the other four went to the spring to fill a kettle and boil some water for tea. By 4 p.m. I had partaken of a light meal of biscuits and tea, which would have to keep me going until next day, and refusing the men's request to be permitted to stay the night in one of the houses in Thak, I sent them back to camp. There was a certain amount of risk in doing this, but it was nothing compared to the risk they would run if they spent the night in Thak.

My seat on the tree consisted of several strands of rope tied between two upright branches, with a couple of strands lower down for my feet to rest on. When I had settled down comfortably I pulled the branches round me and secured them in position with a thin cord, leaving a small opening to see and fire through. My "hide" was soon tested, for shortly after the men had gone the two magpies returned, and attracted others, and nine of them fed on the kill until dusk. The presence of the birds enabled me to get some sleep, for they would have given me warning of the tigress's approach, and with their departure my all-night vigil started.

There was still sufficient daylight to shoot by when the moon, a day off the full, rose over the Nepal hills behind me and flooded the hillside with brilliant light. The rain of the previous night had cleared the atmosphere of dust and smoke and, after the moon had been up a few minutes, the light was so good that I was able to see a sambur and her young one feeding in a field of wheat a hundred and fifty yards away.

The dead buffalo was directly in front and about twenty yards away, and the path along which I expected the tigress to come was two or three yards nearer, so I should have an easy shot at a range at which it would be impossible to miss the tigress—provided she came; and there was no reason why she should not do so.

The moon had been up two hours, and the sambur had approached to within fifty yards of my tree, when a kakar started barking on the hill just above the village. The kakar had been barking for some minutes when suddenly a scream which I can only, very inadequately, describe as "Ar-Ar-Arr", dying away on a long-drawn-out note, came from the direction of the village. So sudden and so unexpected had the scream been that I involuntarily stood up with the intention of slipping down from the tree and dashing up to the village, for the thought flashed through my mind that the man-eater was killing one of my men. Then in a second flash of thought I remembered I had counted them one by one as they had passed my tree, and that I had watched them out of sight on their way back to camp to see if they were obeying my instructions to keep close together.

The scream had been the despairing cry of a human being in mortal agony, and reason questioned how such a sound could have come from a deserted village. It was not a thing of my imagination, for the kakar had heard it and had abruptly stopped barking, and the sambur had dashed away across the fields closely followed by her young one. Two days previously, when I had escorted the men to the village, I had remarked that they appeared to be very confiding to leave their property behind doors that were not even shut or latched, and the Headman had answered that even if their village remained untenanted for years, their property would be quite safe; as long as the tigress lived she was a better guard than any hundred men could be, for no one in all that countryside would dare to approach the village, for any purpose, through the dense forests that surrounded it, unless escorted by me as they had been.

The screams were not repeated, and as there appeared to be nothing that I could do, I settled down again on my rope seat. At 10 p.m. a kakar that was feeding on the young wheat crop at the lower end of the fields dashed away barking, and a minute later the tigress called twice. She had now left the village and was on the move, and even if she did not fancy having another meal off the buffalo, there was every hope of her coming along the path which she had used twice every day for the past few days. With finger on trigger and eyes straining on the path I sat hour after hour until daylight succeeded moonlight; and when the sun had been up an hour, my men returned.

When I got back to camp, I found a number of men sitting near my tent. Among them was the Headman of Thak, and when the others had gone I questioned him about the kill at Thak on the 12th of the month, when he so narrowly escaped falling a victim to the man-eater.

Once again the Headman told me in great detail how he had gone to his fields to dig ginger, taking his grand-child with him, and how on hearing his wife calling he had caught the child's hand and run back to the house—where his wife had said a word or two to him about not keeping his ears open and thereby endangering his own and the child's life—and how a few minutes later the tigress had killed a man while he was cutting leaves off a tree in a field above his house.

All this part of the story I had heard before, and I now asked him if he had actually seen the tigress killing the man. His answer was no; and he added that the tree was not visible from where he had been standing. I then asked him how he knew that the man had been killed, and he said, because he had heard him. In reply to further questions he said the man had not called for help but had cried out; and when asked if he had cried out once he said, "No, three times," and then at my request he gave an imitation of the man's cry. It was the same—but a very modified rendering—as the screams I had heard the previous night.

I then told him what I had heard and asked him if it was possible for anyone to have arrived at the village accidentally, and his answer was an emphatic negative. There were only two paths leading to Thak, and every man, woman, and child in the villages through which these two paths passed knew that Thak was deserted and the reason for its being so. It was known throughout the district that it was dangerous to go near Thak in daylight, and it was therefore quite impossible for anyone to have been in the village at eight o'clock the previous night.

When asked if he could give any explanation for screams having come from a village in which there could not—according to him—have been any human beings, his answer was that he could not. And as I can do no better than the Headman, it were best to assume that neither the kakar, the sambur, nor I heard those very real screams—the screams of a human being in mortal agony.

When I got down from the tree I had one hour in which to get back to camp before dark. Calling up the men, hearing what they had to say, collecting the goats, and walking to the ridge had taken about thirty minutes, and judging from the position of the sun, which was now casting a red glow on the peaks of the Nepal hills, I calculated I had roughly half an hour's daylight in hand. This time factor, or perhaps it would be more correct to say light factor, was all-important, for if I took the opportunity that offered, on it would depend the lives of five men.

The tigress was a mile away, and the intervening ground was densely wooded, strewn over with great rocks, and cut up by a number of deep nullahs, but she could cover the distance well within the half-hour—if she wanted to. The question I had to decide was, whether or not I should try to call her up. If I called and she heard me, and came while it was still daylight and gave me a shot, all would be well; on the other hand, if she came and did not give me a shot some of us would not reach camp, for we had nearly two miles to go, and the path the whole way ran through heavy jungle, and was bordered in some places by big rocks, and in others by dense brushwood. It was useless to consult the men, for none of them had ever been in a jungle before coming on this trip, so the decision would have to be mine. I decided to try to call up the tigress.

Handing my rifle over to one of the men, I waited until the tigress called again and, cupping my hands round my mouth and filling my lungs to their utmost limit, sent an answering call over the valley. Back came her call and thereafter, for several minutes, call answered call. She would come, had in fact already started, and if she arrived while there was light to shoot by, all the advantages would be on my side, for I had the selecting of the ground on which it would best suit me to meet her. November is the mating season for tigers, and it was evident that for the past forty-eight hours she had been rampaging through the jungles in search of a mate, and that now, on hearing what she thought was a tiger answering her mating call, she would lose no time in joining him.

Four hundred yards down the ridge the path runs for fifty yards across a flat bit of ground. At the far right-hand side of this flat ground the path skirts a big rock and then drops steeply, and continues in a series of hairpin bends, down to the next bench. It was at this rock I decided to meet the tigress, and on my way down to it I called several times to let her know I was changing my position, and also to keep in touch with her.

I want you now to have a clear picture of the ground in your mind, to enable you to follow the subsequent events. Imagine, then, a rectangular piece of ground forty yards wide and eighty yards long, ending in a more or less perpendicular rock face. The path coming down from Thak runs on to this ground at its short or south end, and after continuing down the centre for twenty-five yards bends to the right and leaves the rectangle on its long or east side. At the point where the path leaves the flat ground there is a rock about four feet high. From a little beyond where the path bends to the right, a ridge of rock, three or four feet high, rises and extends to the north side of the rectangle, where the ground falls away in a perpendicular rock face. On the near or path side of this low ridge there is a dense line of bushes approaching to

within ten feet of the four-foot-high rock I have mentioned. The rest of the rectangle is grown over with trees,
scattered bushes, and short grass.

It was my intention to lie on the path by the side of the
rock and shoot the tigress as she approached me, but when
I tried this position I found it would not be possible for
me to see her until she was within two or three yards, and
further, that she could get at me either round the rock
or through the scattered bushes on my left without my
seeing her at all. Projecting out of the rock, from the side
opposite to that from which I expected the tigress to
approach, there was a narrow ledge. By sitting sideways I
found I could get a little of my bottom on the ledge, and
by putting my left hand flat on the top of the rounded
rock and stretching out my right leg to its full extent and
touching the ground with my toes, retain my position on
it. The men and goats I placed immediately behind, and
ten to twelve feet below me.

The stage was now set for the reception of the tigress,
who while these preparations were being made had
approached to within three hundred yards. Sending out
one final call to give her direction, I looked round to see
if my men were all right.

The spectacle these men presented would under other
circumstances have been ludicrous, but was here tragic.
Sitting in a tight little circle with their knees drawn up
and their heads together, with the goats burrowing in
under them, they had that look of intense expectancy on
their screwed-up features that one sees on the faces of
spectators waiting to hear a big gun go off. From the
time we had first heard the tigress from the ridge, neither

the men nor the goats had made a sound, beyond one suppressed cough. They were probably by now frozen with fear—as well they might be—and even if they were, I take my hat off to those four men who had the courage to do what I, had I been in their shoes, would not have dreamt of doing. For seven days they had been hearing the most exaggerated and blood-curdling tales of this fearsome beast, and now, while darkness was coming on, and sitting unarmed in a position where they could see nothing, they were listening to the man-eater drawing nearer and nearer; greater courage, and greater faith, it is not possible to conceive.

The fact that I could not hold my rifle, a D.B. 450/400, with my left hand (which I was using to retain my precarious seat on the ledge) was causing me some uneasiness, for apart from the fear of the rifle's slipping on the rounded top of the rock—I had folded my handkerchief and placed the rifle on it to try to prevent this—I did not know what would be the effect of the recoil of a high-velocity rifle fired in this position. The rifle was pointing along the path, in which there was a hump, and it was my intention to fire into the tigress's face immediately it appeared over this hump, which was twenty feet from the rock.

The tigress, however, did not keep to the contour of the hill, which would have brought her out on the path a little beyond the hump, but crossed a deep ravine and came straight towards where she had heard my last call, at an angle which I can best describe as one o'clock. This manoeuvre put the low ridge of rock, over which I could not see, between us. She had located the direction of my last call with great accuracy, but had misjudged the distance, and not finding her prospective mate at the spot she had expected him to be, she was now working herself up into a perfect fury, and you will have some idea of what the fury of a tigress in her condition can be when I tell you that not many miles from my home a tigress on one occasion closed a public road for a whole week, attacking everything that attempted to go along it, including a string of camels, until she was finally joined by a mate.

I know of no sound more liable to fret one's nerves than the calling of an unseen tiger at close range. What effect this appalling sound was having on my men I was frightened to think, and if they had gone screaming down the hill I should not have been at all surprised, for even though I had the heel of a good rifle to my shoulder and the stock against my cheek, I felt like screaming myself.

But even more frightening than this continuous calling was the fading out of the light. Another few seconds, ten or fifteen at the most, and it would be too dark to see my sights, and we should then be at the mercy of a man-eater, plus a tigress wanting a mate. Something would have to be done, and done in a hurry, if we were not to be massacred, and the only thing I could think of was to call.

The tigress was now so close that I could hear the intake of her breath each time before she called, and as she again filled her lungs, I did the same with mine, and we called simultaneously. The effect was startlingly instantaneous. Without a second's hesitation she came tramping with quick steps through the dead leaves, over the low ridge, and into the bushes a little to my right front, and just as I was expecting her to walk right on top of me she stopped, and the next moment the full blast of her deep-throated call struck me in the face and would have carried the hat off my head had I been wearing one. A second's pause, then again quick steps; a glimpse of her as she passed between two bushes, and then she stepped right out into the open, and, looking into my face, stopped dead.

By great and unexpected good luck the half-dozen steps the tigress took to her right front carried her almost to the exact spot at which my rifle was pointing. Had she continued in the direction in which she was coming before her last call, my story—if written—would have had a different ending, for it would have been as impossible to slew the rifle on the rounded top of the rock as it would have been to lift and fire it with one hand.

Owing to the nearness of the tigress, and the fading light, all that I could see of her was her head. My first bullet caught her under the right eye and the second, fired more by accident than with intent, took her in the throat, and she came to rest with her nose against the rock. The recoil from the right barrel loosened my hold on the rock and knocked me off the ledge, and the recoil from the left barrel, fired while I was in the air, brought the rifle up in violent contact with my jaw and sent me heels over head right on top of the men and goats. Once again I take my hat off to those four men, for, not knowing but what the tigress was going to land on them next, they caught me as I fell and saved me from injury and my rifle from being broken.

When I had freed myself from the tangle of human and goat legs I took the ·275 rifle from the man who was holding it, rammed a clip of cartridges into the magazine, and sent a stream of five bullets singing over the valley and across the Sarda into Nepal. Two shots, to the thousands of men in the valley and in the surrounding villages who were anxiously listening for the sound of my rifle, might mean anything, but two shots followed by five more, spaced at regular intervals of five seconds, could only be interpreted as conveying one message, and that was, that the man-eater was dead.

I had not spoken to my men from the time we had first heard the tigress from the ridge. On my telling them now that she was dead and that there was no longer any reason for us to be afraid, they did not appear to be able to take in what I was saying, so I told them to go up and have a look while I found and lit a cigarette. Very cautiously they climbed up to the rock, but went no farther, for, as I have told you, the tigress was touching the other side of it. Late in camp that night, while sitting round a camp-fire and relating their experiences to relays of eager listeners, their narrative invariably ended up with, "and then the tiger whose roaring had turned our livers into water hit the sahib on the head and knocked him down on top of us and if you don't believe us, go and look at his face." A mirror is superfluous in camp, and even if I had had one it could not have made the swelling on my jaw, which put me on milk diet for several days, look as large and as painful as it felt.

By the time a sapling had been felled and the tigress lashed to it, lights were beginning to show in the Ladhya valley and in all the surrounding camps and villages. The four men were very anxious to have the honour of carrying the tigress to camp, but the task was beyond them; so I left them and set off for help.

In my three visits to Chuka during the past eight months I had been along this path many times by day and always with a loaded rifle in my hands, and now I was stumbling down in the dark, unarmed, my only anxiety being to avoid a fall. If the greatest happiness one can experience is the sudden cessation of great pain, then the second greatest happiness is undoubtedly the sudden cessation of great fear. One short hour previously it would have taken wild elephants to have dragged from their homes and camps the men who now, singing and shouting, were converging from every direction, singly and in groups, on the path leading to Thak. Some of the men of this rapidly growing crowd went up the path to help carry in the tigress, while others accompanied me on my way to camp, and would have carried me had I permitted them. Progress was slow, for frequent halts had to be made to allow each group of new arrivals to express their gratitude in their own particular way. This gave the party carrying the tigress time to catch us up, and we entered the village together. I will not attempt to describe the welcome my men and I received, or the scenes I witnessed at Chuka that night.

The Headman of Thak told me he would send word in the morning to the people of Thak to return to their village. This he did, and two days later the entire population returned to their homes, and have lived in peace ever since.

9 *The Chessboard Fields*

GERALD DURRELL

BELOW THE villa, between the line of hills on which it stood and the sea, were the Chessboard Fields. The sea curved into the coast in a great, almost landlocked bay, shallow and bright, and on the flat land along its edges lay the intricate pattern of narrow waterways that had once been salt pans in the Venetian days. Each neat little patch of earth, framed with canals, was richly cultivated and green with crops of maize, potatoes, figs and grapes. These fields, small coloured squares edged with shining waters, lay like a sprawling, multi-coloured chessboard on which the peasants' coloured figures moved from place to place.

One afternoon, having nothing better to do, I decided to take the dogs and visit the fields. I would make yet another attempt to catch Old Plop, cut across to the sea for a feed of cockles and a swim, and make my way home via Petro's land so that I could sit and exchange gossip with him over a water-melon or a few plump pomegranates. Old Plop was a large and ancient terrapin that lived in one of the canals. I had been trying to capture him for a month or more, but in spite of his age he was very wily and quick, and no matter how cautiously I stalked him when he lay asleep on the muddy bank, he would always wake up at the crucial moment, his legs would flail frantically, and he would slide down the mud slope and plop into the water like a corpulent lifeboat being launched. I was determined to possess him, and as I had left him alone for a whole week I thought it was high time to launch another attack.

With my bag of bottles and boxes, my net and a basket to put Old Plop in should I catch him, I set off down the hill with the dogs. Cutting across the first three fields, I paused for a moment in Taki's patch to sample his grapes. He wasn't there, but I knew he wouldn't mind. The dogs and I ate four bunches and I put another two bunches in my collecting bag for future reference, after which we followed the edge of the canal towards the place where Old Plop had his favourite mud slide. As we were drawing near to this spot, I was just about to caution the dogs on the need for absolute silence, when a large green lizard flashed out of a corn-patch and scuttled away. The dogs, barking wildly, galloped in eager pursuit. By the time I reached Old Plop's mud slide there was only a series of gently expanding ripples on the water to tell me that he had been present. I sat down and waited for the dogs to rejoin me, running through in my mind the rich and colourful insults with which I would bombard them. But to my surprise they did not come back. Their yelping in the distance died away, there was a pause, and then they started to bark in a chorus—monotonous, evenly spaced barks that meant they had found something. Wondering what it could be I hurried after them.

They were clustered in a half-circle round a clump of grass at the water's edge, and came gambolling to meet me, tails thrashing, whining with excitement, Roger lifting his upper lip in a pleased grin that I had come to examine

their find. At first I could not see what it was they were so
excited over; then what I had taken to be a rootlet moved,
and I was looking at a pair of fat brown water-snakes,
coiled passionately together in the grass, regarding me
with impersonal silvery eyes from their spade-shaped
heads. This was a thrilling find, and one that almost
compensated for the loss of Old Plop. I had long wanted
to catch one of these snakes, but they were such fast and
skilful swimmers that I had never succeeded in getting
close enough to accomplish a capture. Now the dogs had
found this fine pair, lying in the sun—there for the taking,
as it were.

The dogs, having done their duty by finding these
creatures and leading me to them, now retreated to a safe
distance (for they did not trust reptiles) and sat watching
me interestedly. Slowly I manoeuvred my butterfly net
round until I could unscrew the handle; having done this,
I had a stick with which to do the catching, but the problem was *how* to catch two snakes with one stick? While I
was working this out, one of them decided the thing for
me, uncoiling himself unhurriedly and sliding into the
water as cleanly as a knife-blade. Thinking that I had lost
him, I watched irritably as his undulating length merged
with the water reflection. Then, to my delight, I saw a
column of mud rise slowly through the water and expand
like a rose on the surface; the reptile had buried himself at
the bottom, and I knew he would stay there until he
thought I had gone. I turned my attention to his mate,
pressing her down in the lush grass with the stick; she
twisted herself into a complicated knot, and opening her
pink mouth, hissed at me. I grabbed her firmly round the

neck between finger and thumb, and she hung limp in my hand while I stroked her handsome white belly, and the brown back where the scales were raised slightly like the surface of a fir-cone. I put her tenderly into the basket, and then prepared to capture the other one. I walked a little way down the bank and stuck the handle of the net into the canal to test the depth, and discovered that about two feet of water lay on a three-foot bed of soft, quivering mud. Since the water was opaque, and the snake was buried in the bottom slush, I thought the simplest method would be to feel for him with my toes (as I did when searching for cockles) and, having located him, to make a quick pounce.

I took off my sandals and lowered myself into the warm water, feeling the liquid mud squeeze up between my toes and stroke up my legs, as soft as ashes. Two great black clouds bloomed about my thighs and drifted across the channel. I made my way towards the spot where my quarry lay hidden, moving my feet slowly and carefully in the shifting curtain of mud. Suddenly, under my foot, I felt the slithering body, and I plunged my arms elbow-deep into the water and grabbed. My fingers closed only on mud which oozed between them and drifted away in turbulent, slow-motion clouds. I was just cursing my ill-luck when the snake shot to the surface a yard away from me, and started to swim sinuously along the surface. With a yell of triumph I flung myself full length on top of him.

There was a confused moment as I sank beneath the dark waters and the silt boiled up into my eyes, ears and mouth, but I could feel the reptile's body thrashing wildly to and fro, firmly clasped in my left hand, and I glowed with triumph. Gasping and spluttering under my layer of mud, I sat up in the canal and grabbed the snake round the neck before he could recover his wits and bite me; then I spat for a long time, to rid my teeth and lips of the fine, gritty layer which coated them. When I at last rose to my feet and turned to wade ashore I found to my surprise that my audience of dogs had been enlarged by the silent arrival of a man, who was squatting comfortably on his haunches and watching me with a mixture of interest and amusement.

He was a short, stocky individual whose brown face was topped by a thatch of close-cropped fair hair, the colour of tobacco. He had large, very blue eyes that had a pleasant humorous twinkle in them, and crows' feet in the fine skin at the corners. A short, hawk's-beak nose curved over a wide and humorous mouth. He was wearing a blue cotton shirt that was bleached and faded to the colour of a forget-me-not dried by the sun, and old grey flannel trousers. I did not recognize him, and supposed him to be a fisherman from some village farther down the coast. He regarded me gravely as I scrambled up the bank, and then smiled.

"Your health," he said in a rich, deep voice.

I returned his greeting politely, and then busied myself with the job of trying to get the second snake into the basket without letting the first one escape. I expected him to deliver a lecture to me on the deadliness of the harmless water-snakes and the dangers I ran by handling them, but to my surprise he remained silent, watching with interest while I pushed the writhing reptile into the basket. This done, I washed my hands and produced the grapes I had filched from Taki's fields. The man accepted half the fruit and we sat without talking, sucking the pulp from the grapes with noisy enjoyment. When the last skin had plopped into the canal, the man produced tobacco and rolled a cigarette between his blunt, brown fingers.

"You are a stranger?" he asked, inhaling deeply and with immense satisfaction.

I said that I was English, and that I and my family lived in a villa up in the hills. Then I waited for the inevitable questions as to the sex, number and age of my family, their work and aspirations, followed by a skilful cross-examination as to why we lived in Corfu. This was the usual peasant way; it was not done unpleasantly, nor with any motive other than friendly interest. They would vouchsafe their own private business to you with great simplicity and frankness, and would be hurt if you did not do the same. But, to my surprise, the man seemed satisfied with my answer, and asked nothing further, but sat there blowing fine streamers of smoke into the sky and staring about him with dreamy blue eyes. With my finger-nail I scraped an attractive pattern in the hardening carapace of grey mud on my thigh, and decided that I would have to go down to the sea and wash both myself and my clothes before returning home. I got to my feet and shouldered my bag and nets; the dogs got to their feet, shook themselves and yawned. More out of politeness than anything, I asked the man where he was going. It was, after all, peasant etiquette to ask questions. It showed your interest in the person. So far I hadn't asked him anything at all.

"I'm going down to the sea," he said, gesturing with his cigarette—"down to my boat. . . . Where are you going?"

I said I was making for the sea too, first to wash and secondly to find some cockles to eat.

"I will walk with you," he said, rising and stretching. "I have a basketful of cockles in my boat; you may have some of those if you like."

We walked through the fields in silence, and when we came out on to the sands he pointed at the distant shape of a rowing-boat, lying comfortably on her side, with a frilly skirt of ripples round her stern. As we walked towards her I asked if he was a fisherman, and if so, where he came from.

"I come from here . . . from the hills," he replied—"at least, my home is here, but I am now at Vido."

The reply puzzled me, for Vido was a tiny islet lying off the town of Corfu, and as far as I knew it had no one on it at all except convicts and warders, for it was the local prison island. I pointed this out to him.

"That's right," he agreed, stooping to pat Roger as he ambled past, "that's right. I'm a convict."

I thought he was joking, and glanced at him sharply, but his expression was quite serious. I said I presumed he had just been let out.

"No, no, worse luck," he smiled. "I have another two years to do. But I'm a good prisoner, you see. Trustworthy and make no trouble. Any like me, those they feel they can trust, are allowed to make boats and sail home for the week-end, if it's not too far. I've got to be back there first thing Monday morning."

Once the thing was explained, of course, it was simple. It never even occurred to me that the procedure was unusual. I knew one wasn't allowed home for week-ends from an English prison, but this was Corfu, and in Corfu anything could happen. I was bursting with curiosity to know what his crime had been, and I was just phrasing a tactful inquiry in my mind when we reached the boat, and inside it was something that drove all other thoughts from my head. In the stern, tethered to the seat by one yellow leg, sat an immense black-backed gull, who contemplated me with sneering yellow eyes. I stepped forward eagerly and stretched out my hand to the broad, dark back.

"Be careful . . . watch out; he is a bully, that one!" said the man urgently.

His warning came too late, for I had already placed my hand on the bird's back and was gently running my fingers over the silken feathering. The gull crouched, opened his beak slightly, and the dark iris of his eye contracted with surprise, but he was so taken aback by my audacity that he did nothing.

"Spiridion!" said the man in amazement, "he must like you, he's never let anyone else touch him without biting."

I buried my fingers in the crisp white feathers on the bird's neck, and as I scratched gently the gull's head drooped forwards and his yellow eyes became dreamy. I asked the man where he had managed to catch such a magnificent bird.

"I sailed over to Albania in the spring to try to get some hares, and I found him in a nest. He was small then, and fluffy as a lamb. Now he's like a great duck," the man said, staring pensively at the gull, "fat duck, ugly duck, biting duck, aren't you, eh?"

The gull at being thus addressed opened one eye and

gave a short, harsh yarp, which may have been repudi-
ation or agreement. The man leant down and pulled a big
basket from under the seat; it was full to the brim with
great fat cockles that chinked musically. We sat in the
boat and ate the shellfish, and all the time I watched the
bird, fascinated by the snow-white breast and head, his
long hooked beak and fierce eyes, as yellow as spring
crocuses, the broad back and powerful wings, sooty black.
From the soles of his great webbed feet to the tip of his
beak he was, in my opinion, quite admirable. I swallowed
a final cockle, wiped my hands on the side of the boat and
asked the man if he could get a baby gull for me the
following spring.

"You want one?" he said in surprise; "you like them?"

I felt this was understating my feelings. I would have
sold my soul for such a gull.

"Well, have him if you want him," said the man casually, jerking a thumb at the bird.

I could hardly believe my ears. For someone to possess
such a wonderful creature and to offer him as a gift so
carelessly was incredible. Didn't he *want* the bird, I asked?

"Yes, I like him," said the man, looking at the bird
meditatively, "but he eats more than I can catch for him,
and he is such a wicked one that he bites everybody; none
of the other prisoners or the warders like him. I've tried
letting him go, but he *won't* go—he keeps coming back.
I was going to take him over to Albania one week-end and
leave him there. So if you're sure you want him you can
have him."

Sure I wanted him? It was like being offered an angel.
A slightly sardonic-looking angel, it's true, but one with

the most magnificent wings. In my excitement I never even stopped to wonder how the family would greet the arrival of a bird the size of a goose with a beak like a razor. In case the man changed his mind I hastily took off my clothes, beat as much of the dried mud off them as possible, and had a quick swim in the shallows. I put on my clothes again, whistled the dogs, and prepared to carry my prize home. The man untied the string, lifted the gull up and handed him to me; I clasped it under one arm, surprised that such a huge bird should be so feather-light. I thanked the man profusely for his wonderful present.

"He knows his name," he remarked, clasping the gull's beak between his fingers and waggling it gently. "I call him Alecko. He'll come when you call."

Alecko, on hearing his name, paddled his feet wildly and looked up into my face with questioning yellow eyes.

"You'll be wanting some fish for him," remarked the man. "I'm going out in the boat tomorrow, about eight. If you like to come we can catch a good lot for him."

I said that would be fine, and Alecko gave a yarp of agreement. The man leant against the bows of the boat to push it out, and I suddenly remembered something. As casually as I could I asked him what his name was, and why he was in prison. He smiled charmingly over his shoulder.

"My name's Kosti," he said, "Kosti Panopoulos. I killed my wife."

He leant against the bows of the boat and heaved; she slid whispering across the sand and into the water, and the little ripples leapt and licked at her stern, like excited puppies. Kosti scrambled into the boat and took up the oars.

"Your health," he called. "Until tomorrow."

The oars creaked musically, and the boat skimmed rapidly over the limpid waters. I turned, clasping my precious bird under my arm, and started to trudge back over the sand, towards the chessboard fields.

The walk home took me some time. I decided that I had misjudged Alecko's weight, for he appeared to get heavier and heavier as we progressed. He was a dead weight that sagged lower and lower, until I was forced to jerk him up under my arm again, whereupon he would protest with a vigorous yarp. We were half way through the fields when I saw a convenient fig tree which would, I thought, provide both shade and sustenance, so I decided to take a rest. While I lay in the long grass and munched figs, Alecko sat nearby as still as though he were carved out of wood, watching the dogs with unblinking eyes. The only sign of life were his irises, which would expand and contract excitedly each time one of the dogs moved.

Presently, rested and refreshed, I suggested to my band that we tackle the last stage of the journey; the dogs rose obediently, but Alecko fluffed out his feathers so that they rustled like dry leaves, and shuddered all over at the thought. Apparently he disapproved of my hawking him around under my arm like an old sack, ruffling his feathers. Now that he had persuaded me to put him down in such a pleasant spot he had no intention of continuing what appeared to him to be a tedious and unnecessary journey. As I stooped to pick him up he snapped his beak, uttered a loud, harsh scream, and lifted his wings above his back in the posture usually adopted by tombstone angels. He glared at me. Why, his look seemed to imply, leave this spot? There was shade, soft grass to sit on, and water nearby; what point was there in leaving it to be humped about the countryside in a manner both uncomfortable and undignified? I pleaded with him for some time, and, as he appeared to have calmed down, I made another attempt to pick him up. This time he left me in no doubt as to his desire to stay where he was. His beak shot out so fast I could not avoid it, and it hit my approaching hand accurately. It was as though I had been slashed by an ice-pick. My knuckles were bruised and aching, and a two-inch gash welled blood in great profusion. Alecko looked so smug and satisfied with this attack that I lost my temper. Grabbing my butterfly net I brought it down skilfully and, to his surprise, enveloped him in its folds. I jumped on him before he could recover from the shock and grabbed his beak in one hand. Then I wrapped my handkerchief round and round his beak and tied it securely in place with a bit of string, after which I took off my shirt and wrapped it round him, so that his flailing wings were pinioned tightly to his body. He lay there, trussed up as though for market, glaring at me and uttering muffled screams of rage. Grimly I picked up my equipment, put him under my arm and stalked off towards home. Having got the gull, I wasn't going to stand any nonsense about getting him back to the villa. For the rest of the journey Alecko proceeded to produce, uninterruptedly, a series of wild, strangled cries of piercing quality, so by the time we reached the house I was thoroughly angry with him.

I stamped into the drawing-room, put Alecko on the floor and started to unwrap him, while he accompanied the operation raucously. The noise brought Mother and Margo hurrying in from the kitchen. Alecko, now freed from my shirt, stood in the middle of the room with the handkerchief still tied round his beak and trumpeted furiously.

"What on earth's that?" gasped Mother.

"What an *enormous* bird!" exclaimed Margo. "What is it, an eagle?"

My family's lack of ornithological knowledge had always been a source of annoyance to me. I explained testily that it was not an eagle but a black-backed gull, and told them how I had got him.

"But, dear, how on earth are we going to *feed* him?" asked Mother. "Does he eat fish?"

Alecko, I said hopefully, would eat anything. I tried to catch him to remove the handkerchief from his beak, but he was obviously under the impression that I was trying to attack him, so he screamed and trumpeted loudly and ferociously through the handkerchief. This fresh outburst brought Larry and Leslie down from their rooms.

"Who the hell's playing *bagpipes*?" demanded Larry as he swept in.

Alecko paused for a moment, surveyed this newcomer coldly, and, having summed him up, yarped loudly and scornfully.

"My God!" said Larry, backing hastily and bumping into Leslie. "What the devil's *that*?"

"It's a new bird Gerry's got," said Margo; "doesn't it look *fierce*?"

"It's a gull," said Leslie, peering over Larry's shoulder; "what a whacking great thing!"

"Nonsense," said Larry; "it's an albatross."

"No, it's a gull."

"Don't be silly. Whoever saw a gull that size? I tell you it's a bloody great albatross."

Alecko padded a few paces towards Larry and yarped at him again.

"Call him off," Larry commanded. "Gerry, get the damn thing under *control*; it's attacking me."

"Just stand still. He won't hurt you," advised Leslie.

"It's all very well for you; you're behind me. Gerry, catch that bird at once, before it does me irreparable damage."

"Don't shout so, dear; you'll frighten it."

"I like that! A thing like a Roc flapping about on the floor attacking everyone, and you tell me not to frighten it."

I managed to creep up behind Alecko and grab him; then, amid his deafening protests, I removed the handkerchief from his beak. When I let him go again he shuddered indignantly, and snapped his beak two or three times with a sound like a whip-crack.

"Listen to it!" exclaimed Larry. "Gnashing its teeth!"

"They haven't got teeth," observed Leslie.

"Well, it's gnashing *something*. I hope you're not going to let him keep it, Mother? It's obviously a dangerous brute; look at its eyes. Besides, it's unlucky."

"Why unlucky?" asked Mother, who had a deep interest in superstition.

"It's a well-known thing. Even if you have just the *feathers* in the house everyone goes down with plague, or goes mad or something."

"That's peacocks you're thinking of, dear."

"No, I tell you it's albatrosses. It's well known."

"No, dear, it's peacocks that are unlucky."

"Well, anyway, we can't have that thing in the house. It would be sheer lunacy. Look what happened to the Ancient Mariner. We'll all have to sleep with crossbows under our pillows."

"Really, Larry, you do *complicate* things," said Mother. "It seems quite tame to me."

"You wait until you wake up one morning and find you've had your eyes gouged out."

"What nonsense you talk, dear. It looks quite harmless."

At this moment Dodo, who always took a little while to catch up with rapidly moving events, noticed Alecko for the first time. Breathing heavily, her eyes protruding with interest, she waddled forward and sniffed at him. Alecko's beak flashed out, and if Dodo had not turned her head at that moment—in response to my cry of alarm—her nose would have been neatly sliced off; as it was she received a glancing blow on the side of the head that surprised her so much that her leg leapt out of joint. She threw back her head and let forth a piercing yell. Alecko, evidently under the impression that it was a sort of vocal contest, did his best to out-scream Dodo, and flapped his wings so vigorously that he blew out the nearest lamp.

"There you are," said Larry in triumph. "What did I say? Hasn't been in the house five minutes and it kills the dog."

Mother and Margo massaged Dodo back to silence, and Alecko sat and watched the operation with interest. He clicked his beak sharply, as if astonished at the frailty of the dog tribe, decorated the floor lavishly and wagged his tail with the swagger of one who had done something clever.

"How nice!" said Larry. "Now we're expected to wade about the house waist deep in guano."

"Hadn't you better take him outside, dear?" suggested Mother. "Where are you going to keep him?"

I said that I had thought of dividing the Magenpies' cage and keeping Alecko there. Mother said this was a very good idea. Until his cage was ready I tethered him on the veranda, warning each member of the family in turn as to his whereabouts.

"Well," observed Larry as we sat over dinner, "don't blame *me* if the house is hit by a cyclone. I've warned you; I can do no more."

"Why a cyclone, dear?"

"Albatrosses always bring bad weather with them."

"It's the first time I've heard a cyclone described as bad weather," observed Leslie.

"But it's *peacocks* that are unlucky, dear; I keep telling you," Mother said plaintively. "I know, because an aunt of mine had some of the tail-feathers in the house and the cook died."

"My dear Mother, the albatross is world famous as a bird of ill-omen. Hardened old salts are known to go white and faint when they see one. I tell you, we'll find the chimney covered with Saint Elmo's fire one night, and before we know where we are we'll be drowned in our beds by a tidal wave."

"You said it would be a cyclone," Margo pointed out.

"A cyclone *and* a tidal wave," said Larry, "with probably a touch of earthquake and volcanic eruptions thrown in. It's tempting Providence to keep that beast."

"Where did you get him, anyway?" Leslie asked me.

I explained about my meeting with Kosti (omitting any mention of the water-snakes, for all snakes were taboo with Leslie) and how he had given me the bird.

"Nobody in their right senses would give somebody a present like that," observed Larry. "Who is this man, anyway?"

Without thinking, I said he was a convict.

"A *convict?*" quavered Mother. "What d'you mean, a convict?"

I explained about Kosti being allowed home for the week-ends, because he was a trusted member of the Vido community. I added that he and I were going fishing the next morning.

"I don't know whether it's very wise, dear," Mother said doubtfully. "I don't like the idea of your going about with a convict. You never know what he's done."

Indignantly, I said I knew perfectly well what he'd done. He killed his wife.

"A *murderer?*" said Mother, aghast. "But what's he doing wandering round the countryside? Why didn't they hang him?"

"They don't have the death penalty here for anything except bandits," explained Leslie; "you get three years for murder and five years if you're caught dynamiting fish."

"Ridiculous!" said Mother indignantly. "I've never heard of anything so scandalous."

"I think it shows a nice sense of the importance of things," said Larry. "Whitebait before women."

"Anyway, I won't have you wandering around with a murderer," said Mother to me. "He might cut your throat or something."

After an hour's arguing and pleading I finally got Mother to agree that I should go fishing with Kosti, providing that Leslie came down and had a look at him first. So the next morning I went fishing with Kosti, and when we returned with enough food to keep Alecko occupied for a couple of days, I asked my friend to come up to the villa, so that Mother could inspect him for herself.

Mother had, after considerable mental effort, managed to commit to memory two or three Greek words. This lack of vocabulary had a restrictive effect on her conversation at the best of times, but when she was faced with the ordeal of exchanging small talk with a murderer she promptly forgot all the Greek she knew. So she had to sit on the veranda, smiling nervously, while Kosti in his faded shirt and tattered pants drank a glass of beer, and while I translated his conversation.

"He seems such a *nice* man," Mother said, when Kosti had taken his leave; "he doesn't look a bit like a murderer."

"What did you think a murderer looked like?" asked Larry—"someone with a hare lip and a club foot, clutching a bottle marked POISON in one hand?"

"Don't be silly, dear; of course not. But I thought he'd look . . . well, you know, a little more *murderous*."

"You simply can't judge by physical appearance," Larry pointed out; "you can only tell by a person's actions. I could have told you he was a murderer at once."

"How, dear?" asked Mother, very intrigued.

"Elementary," said Larry with a deprecating sigh. "No one but a murderer would have thought of giving Gerry that albatross."

10 *The Laird and the Fawn*

DAVID STEPHEN

A**T NOON** the birch leaves wilted and curled inwards with the blast-furnace heat of the sun, and even the heather tips drooped. The deer, tortured by the hot gusts of air, panted audibly, with tongues lolling and flanks heaving. The fawns' coats, sheened and silky with much scorching, showed vague outlines of their vanished spots in the harsh light. The doe rose when Dance, greatly distressed by the relentless heat, tried to bury herself in the heather, and set off in the direction of Firknowe Spinney with all three at her heels.

The hoodie on his grouse butt saw the roebuck herd

approaching, and kwarped his greeting, puffing his throat and lowering his head. The doe ignored his comments, though she should have listened to his advice, for when Smoky Joe gave warnings all wise things lent their ears. At the moment she had no interest in him. Apart from respect for his judgement, she felt only distrust, for she knew the hoodie would peck the eyes from a new-born fawn or take her own if she were ailing. But Joe was well fed, and in bantering mood, and danced on his perch like a buffoon to show he had no evil intentions.

At that moment a dog barked in Firknowe. The crow stopped clowning and the doe pricked her ears. Bounce, his slim legs dusty with yellow pollen, copied her pose and stamped with a foot. The crow, dismissing the sound, said *Harr-rr* to show it was of no importance. But, to the doe, the barking meant a change of plans. Firknowe was now out of the question, yet she was reluctant to lead her fawns across two gruelling miles of heather to reach the ample shade of Glencryan or Dryflatts. It was Bounce who solved her dilemma, by walking into the butt and throwing himself down in the shade of a heather wall buttressed with peat and branches.

Smoky Joe, with head cocked and eyes shining like ripe blackberries, watched intently while they scraped with forehooves to prepare their lies. Dance joined Bounce on the inside, pounding at woody heather twigs, charred with old fires, till she had cleared a patch for her hip. When the doe and Skip were settled, muzzle to muzzle on the outside, Smoky Joe sidled round the top of the butt till he was above Bounce's head. He poked his ebony pick-axe beak between his feet and chuckled in his throat. With neck feathers on end, he pulled silver-crusted tips of dead heather from between his black toes, vibrating his tail as he did so. Then he flew down beside Bounce and said *Kwarp*: *ha-harr*.

Bounce shrank away, not because he was afraid, but because he had a strong ancestral suspicion of all crows, and wanted room to manoeuvre in case of attack. But when the old crow treated him to an elaborate display he reached out to smell him. With beak to ground and breast feathers puffed over his toes, the bird chortled and chuckled, with lifted wings and spread tail vibrating rapidly, as a hen owl does when her mate brings prey to the nest in the night. Bounce watched wide-eyed till Smoky Joe stopped to shake himself, then touched the bird's ash-grey breast with his muzzle. The crow leaped back squawking at the contact, and Bounce jumped to his feet, lowering his head in challenge.

Joe *kwarped* mockingly before dancing away to poke in a corner of the butt, grumbling in his throat as he thrust his glossy head into the packed, brittle heather. Presently he pulled out a piece of rotten mutton, one of many he had hidden in the butt for future use, for the old crow was provident and, unlike the squirrels, remembered all his hiding-places. With his mouth full of mutton, he looked up to find Bounce prodding air, with hindlegs braced as if he was meeting resistance. After much elaborate bowing and tail fanning Joe dropped his titbit, then crouched down behind it like a dog that seeks a quarrel over a bone.

Getting no response to his taunt, he skipped over suddenly and nipped Bounce on a foreleg. Bounce retaliated by mincing forward with head held low; but when he tried to prod he was promptly tweaked in an ear. But this time the crow had gone too far; for the fawn, stung to anger, reared up and struck out with a forehoof. Had the stroke made contact, Smoky Joe would have been a cripple, for that tiny hoof had an edge like a knife. Instead, it merely bent his tail feathers, so he flapped up to the top of the butt before the deer could strike again.

With his tormentor out of reach, Bounce went round behind the butt to seek solace in the company of his mother. He found her sleeping on her side, with legs outstretched, her flanks rising and falling in rhythm with her breathing. Skip, too, was asleep, with his muzzle resting on his mother's hocks. Bounce licked the doe's white chin till she opened her eyes and withdrew her leg from under Skip's chin. Then she rose to give them suck, while the crow, once more inside the butt, went through the ritual of hiding his mutton, wedging it in a corner and covering it with a tiny heap of dry peat, heather stems, and crusted lichen.

After thirty seconds the doe took two steps forward, thus forcing the fawns' heads from under her. Bounce stepped back as Smoky Joe trailed low over the heather, to pitch, squawking, beside a ditch less than thirty yards away. With a vigorous shake of his head the fawn gave chase, jumping six feet to the left, then six to the right, and kicking his heels with his head held low. He found Smoky Joe perched on the exposed ribs of a long-dead sheep. Green, frayed wool clung matted to ribs bleached by weathering and discoloured by the feet of many birds, and two horns were showing above the green slime on the peaty water.

The crow was holding in his beak a black-and-orange beetle which he had picked from the body of the sheep. Scores of other beetles were working under the braxie, trying to undermine it before they laid their eggs in the flesh. Joe crushed his captive as he turned to face the fawn, and swallowed it without distaste; which showed how little he thought of theories, for sexton beetles are supposed to be unpalatable and strikingly coloured to protect them from attack.

Bounce lowered his head, pranced, and launched himself at the crow. He was no longer angry, but prepared to play rough. The hoodie, over-confident, left his evading jump too late, and was struck before his wings had got a grip on the air. But he was allowed to recover when Bounce danced back to work up to a second assault. When the second rush came he was inside the braxie's ribs sorting out his wits. When Bounce made the mistake of sniffing too close he was bitten savagely on the chin, which made him realize that he had no answer to a crow's beak stabbing through the open ribs of a sheep. So he went back to his mother, his inborn distrust of all hoodies confirmed by painful experience.

In the shade of the butt he lay chewing cud, close to his mother with his rump against Skip's flank, while gauzy-winged bees whined past in a constant stream, carrying the heather harvest to the long line of hives on the flat loch shore. His cud chewing was methodical—two movements of the lower jaw to the right, and the remainder to the left, till the mouthful was swallowed. When the next mouthful came up, showing as a ripple on the satin skin of his neck, he repeated the process. At regular intervals of six or seven regurgitations he changed the order, chewing first to the left instead of the right; but the number was always the same—two in one direction, the remainder on the other side.

He was licking his shoulder when Smoky Joe flapped down at the entrance to the butt. But this time the crow was nervous, and his nervousness was somehow conveyed to Bounce's mother, for she jumped suddenly to her feet with head high and ears cupped forward. The crow snipped yellow flowers of tormentil and tossed them over his shoulder, then, with a harsh caw, flew low over the heather towards the stunted pines of Hoolet Nest. The fawns watched the doe, tensed to break; but still she stood, head up, ears twitching, sensing peril yet unable to identify or place it.

Then, suddenly, the tension was broken. The doe barked urgently, and broke away. Behind her a covey of red grouse exploded into the air, to come hurtling after her in tight formation on down-curved wings. Shotguns roared as three men with dogs appeared over a rise a hundred yards from the butt. Two grouse faltered in flight, flapped wings broken with No. 5 shot, and fell on a slant; a third towered and crumpled, beak to breast, before pitching down to hit the heather in a cloud of feathers. The rest of the pack whirred close on the heels of the fleeing deer, almost breasting the heather tops, while the spaniels were waved out to collect dead and find wounded.

But one of the springers, seeing the deer, had a mind to chase them, and raced after them yelping, while men swore and blew recalls in vain. Heat and high heather soon tired the dog, and he turned when he realized he had no hope of catching the deer. While he sneaked back, to be cuffed and sent out to quest, the deer bounded in headlong flight towards Hoolet Nest, with the fawns following in line behind the doe. The ground was new to them, so they ran in her slots. Round dubs of peat, over lichened, heather-crowned boulders, across treacherous water channels topped with sphagnum, the waywise doe led her family without faltering. And presently they reached the great sheugh that bordered the rush-grown Hoolet Nest pastures.

The sheugh or great ditch, deep, with sheer peat sides, was four feet wide and no obstacle to deer that knew the ground. But in front of it the ground rose to a foot-high bank half as wide as the sheugh. The doe jumped from the bank top, sailed up and over, and touched down on the far side with three feet to spare. From the spot slotted by her take-off Bounce leaped unhesitatingly, with forehooves held to his breast and hind legs rigid after the thrust. Landing with inches to spare, he bounded after the doe without slackening pace. Close behind him jumped Dance, who stumbled as she landed. She was on her feet when Skip left the ground. The doe, halting to make sure her fawns were following, saw two running her line, then heard a wild cry from the third; for Skip was in the ditch, having jumped too soon because he thought he had only the bank to clear.

Alarmed, the doe turned back, with white flag spread. From the lip of the sheugh she looked down on her fawn, standing neck deep in dark, peaty water, and wailing piteously like a hare in a snare or in the grip of a collie's teeth. The fawn leaped at sight of his mother furrowing the wet peat with his forehooves; but the ditch was too deep and he fell over backwards with his head under water. Struggling to his feet with much splashing, he coughed the water from his lungs, while the doe, pawing at the top, sent down showers of dry peat that blinded him.

In a panic the doe started to trot along the bank. Skip, afraid she was deserting him, tried to keep pace, plunging and leaping and falling, gulping water when he fell, coughing and drooling when he rose. Peat flinders swirled in the dark, cool water; a fat water vole, nibbling at a rush stem on a narrow spit of peat, fled from the disturbance, escaping to its burrow near the top by tracks no deer could follow.

The doe turned where the sheugh was spanned by a little bridge built of turves and birch poles, which was a crossing place used by foxes. Retracing her steps at a smarter pace, she reached her starting-place, and turned again. And so she carried on, rushing up and down, always turning at the bridge of turf. If she had kept for a hundred yards she could have got the fawn out where the ground was level and the ditch no more than a ribbon of water. But, like a hen confronted with a barrier of netting, she galloped up and down on a short beat, till the fawn in the ditch was exhausted and barely able to keep his head above the water.

Skip was trapped, for he was only a little fawn, twenty inches high at the shoulder, standing helpless in two feet of water, with three feet of sheer ditch wall above him. To the August drought he owed his life, for in normal seasons the rains spilled five feet of chill water into the sheugh, and death would have been a matter of seconds. As it was, he was barely able to stand; he was choking and glassy of eye; and his mother was quite unable to help him.

Men and dogs walking towards the bridge of turf, with three grouse in the game bag and two spaniels casting ahead, sent the doe's ears up when she had made her twentieth run along the sheugh. Men were the last things she could have wished for at that moment, yet they were the only beings able to help her fawn. But such understanding was beyond the powers of the doe, who saw in them only additional peril. So she barked, with flag spread full, and trotted away a little distance, with Bounce and Dance at her side.

The doe started running in circles as the men approached the sheugh, while Bounce and Dance dropped to the ground in obedience to her gruff bark of command. Skip, wailing heartbrokenly, attracted the dogs, and the dogs, barking their discovery to the men, raced to the sheugh. In her frenzy of fear the doe cut in closer, till she was running her circle barely sixty yards from the dogs, barking her summons to a fawn who couldn't follow.

John Long, the keeper, wearing a braw suit of tweeds and a shirt of Cameron tartan, was the first to reach the sheugh. Laying down the game bag, he called off the dogs, and coupled them before looking into the ditch. When he lay down on his belly to peer over the edge, the fawn stood still, shilpet and shivering, and too weak to move.

Long called to his shooting companions to hurry and lend a hand, while the dogs, bobbing on their seats, were warned "Down! Damn ye! Down!"

"A roe kid droonin' in the sheugh," he said, when his

son Willie arrived with the laird. "If ye tak me by the feet I'll mebbe manage tae fish it oot."

So they held him by the ankles, and lowered him over the edge. Long's shirt and green tweed jacket were plastered with wet peat before he got his hands on the fawn. Skip, almost indifferent to the touch, allowed himself to be pulled by the neck, then grasped by the forelegs. Only when he was hoisted from the ditch, held firmly in John Long's arms, did he strike out with a forefoot in a last despairing struggle. The blow took the keeper on the cheek, bruising the bone and cutting the skin, which bled on the instant.

"Damn!" said Long, hurriedly dropping the fawn. "I should hae kent better!"

"That might have been your eye . . ." the laird began. "Take care Willie," he shouted, as the boy knelt to grasp the fawn by the legs. But there was no need for care, for Skip was lying on his side, his tongue protruding from the side of his mouth, his lip drawn back from his lower teeth, his breathing a snort, and his mouth oozing water.

"Look at the auld deer," said Willie, pointing to the doe, who was still bounding on her anxious circuit, barking at intervals.

"Well, sir," said Long to the laird, "this beast's aboot loused. Micht as well chap it on the heid noo and be done wi' it. It'll make grand bait for foxes and hoodies."

The laird turned Skip over with his foot, and found the slim body slack. "Leave it to her," he said at last, "then she'll know. You can do what you like with it in the morning."

But Long was stubborn. "As you say, sir," he said, "but

if the foxes come on it the nicht there'll be little mair than banes gin daylight."

The laird, however, was insistent. The doe didn't know her fawn was dead, and the laird, being a man of some imagination and understanding, wanted to leave her to certainty and mourning. Long, who was a remarkable man in many ways, lacked the finer nuances of imagination, and thought the laird was being stubborn. His son, quite frankly, though he was daft, although he didn't say so.

So they left, with the dogs in hand, walking quickly to allow the doe to tryst with her dead.

Yet, if they could have been present half an hour later, they would have witnessed a strange scene when the doe returned to her fawn. Standing over him, she made low noises in her throat, then gently licked his soaking muzzle. Twice she snorted in his face, all the while tapping him lightly with a caressing, polished forehoof, as if bidding him rise and follow. And, if they had been present later still, they would have seen her, as Kyack saw her, when she entered the Hoolet Nest pines with three fawns at foot.

11 *The Dog that Bit People*

JAMES THURBER

PROBABLY NO one man should have as many dogs in his life as I have had, but there was more pleasure than distress in them for me except in the case of an Airedale named Muggs. He gave me more trouble than all the other fifty-four or five put together, although my moment of keenest embarrassment was the time a Scotch terrier named Jeannie, who had just had six puppies in the clothes closet of a fourth-floor apartment in New York, had the unexpected seventh and last at the corner of Eleventh Street and Fifth Avenue during a walk she had insisted on taking. Then, too, there was the prize-

winning French poodle, a great big black poodle—none of
your little, untroublesome white miniatures—who got
sick riding in the rumble seat of a car with me on her way
to the Greenwich Dog Show. She had a red rubber bib
tucked around her throat and, since a rainstorm came up
when we were halfway through the Bronx, I had to hold
over her a small green umbrella, really more of a parasol.
The rain beat down fearfully, and suddenly the driver of
the car drove into a big garage, filled with mechanics. It
happened so quickly that I forgot to put the umbrella
down, and I will always remember, with sickening distress, the look of incredulity mixed with hatred that came
over the face of the particular hardened garage man that
came over to see what we wanted, when he took a look at
me and the poodle. All garage men, and people of that
intolerant stripe, hate poodles with their curious haircut,
especially the pom-poms that you have got to leave on
their hips if you expect the dogs to win a prize.

But the Airedale, as I have said, was the worst of all my
dogs. He really wasn't my dog, as a matter of fact: I came
home from a vacation one summer to find that my brother
Roy had bought him while I was away. A big, burly,
choleric dog, he always acted as if he thought I wasn't
one of the family. There was a slight advantage in being
one of the family, for he didn't bite the family as often as
he bit strangers. Still, in the years that we had him he bit
everybody but mother, and he made a pass at her once but
missed. That was during the month when we suddenly
had mice, and Muggs refused to do anything about them.
Nobody ever had mice exactly like the mice we had
that month. They acted like pet mice, almost like mice

somebody had trained. They were so friendly that one night when mother entertained at dinner the Friraliras, a club she and my father had belonged to for twenty years, she put down a lot of little dishes with food in them on the pantry floor so that the mice would be satisfied with that and wouldn't come into the dining-room. Muggs stayed out in the pantry with the mice, lying on the floor, growling to himself—not at the mice, but about all the people in the next room that he would have liked to get at. Mother slipped out into the pantry once to see how everything was going. Everything was going fine. It made her so mad to see Muggs lying there, oblivious of the mice— they came running up to her—that she slapped him and he slashed at her, but didn't make it. He was sorry immediately, mother said. He was always sorry, she said, after he bit someone, but we could not understand how she figured this out. He didn't act sorry.

Mother used to send a box of candy every Christmas to the people the Airedale bit. The list finally contained forty or more names. Nobody could understand why we didn't get rid of the dog. I didn't understand it very well myself, but we didn't get rid of him. I think that one or two people tried to poison Muggs—he acted poisoned once in a while—and old Major Moberly fired at him once with his service revolver near the Seneca Hotel in East Broad Street—but Muggs lived to be almost eleven years old, and even when he could hardly get around he bit a Congressman who called to see my father on business. My mother had never liked the Congressman—she said the signs of his horoscope showed he couldn't be trusted (he was Saturn with the moon in Virgo)—but she sent him a box of candy that Christmas. He sent it right back, probably because he suspected it was trick candy. Mother persuaded herself it was all for the best that the dog had bitten him, even though father lost an important business association because of it. "I wouldn't be associated with such a man," mother said, "Muggs could read him like a book."

We used to take turns feeding Muggs to be on his good side, but that didn't always work. He was never in a very good humour, even after a meal. Nobody knew exactly what was the matter with him, but whatever it was it made him irascible, especially in the mornings. Roy never felt very well in the morning, either, especially before break-fast, and once when he came downstairs and found that Muggs had moodily chewed up the morning paper he hit him in the face with a grapefruit and then jumped up on the dining-room table, scattering dishes and silverware and spilling the coffee. Muggs' first free leap carried him all the way across the table and into a brass fire screen in front of the gas grate, but he was back on his feet in a moment, and in the end he got Roy and gave him a pretty vicious bite in the leg. Then he was all over it; he never bit anyone more than once at a time. Mother always mentioned that as an argument in his favour; she said he had a quick temper, but that he didn't hold a grudge. She was for ever defending him. I think she liked him because he wasn't well. "He's not strong," she would say pityingly, but that was inaccurate; he may not have been well, but he was terribly strong.

One time my mother went to the Chittenden Hotel to call on a woman mental healer who was lecturing in

Columbus on the subject of "Harmonious Vibrations". She wanted to find out if it was possible to get harmonious vibrations into a dog. "He's a large tan-coloured Airedale," mother explained. The woman said that she had never treated a dog, but she advised my mother to hold the thought that he did not bite and would not bite. Mother was holding the thought the very next morning when Muggs got the iceman, but she blamed that slip-up on the iceman. "If you didn't think he would bite you, he wouldn't," mother told him. He stomped out of the house in a terrible jangle of vibrations.

One morning when Muggs bit me slightly, more or less in passing, I reached down and grabbed his short, stumpy tail and hoisted him into the air. It was a foolhardy thing to do, and the last time I saw my mother, about six months ago, she said she didn't know what possessed me. I don't either, except that I was pretty mad. As long as I held the dog off the floor by his tail he couldn't get at me, but he twisted and jerked so, snarling all the time, that I realized I couldn't hold him that way very long. I carried him to the kitchen and flung him on to the floor and shut the door on him just as he crashed against it. But I forgot about the back-stairs. Muggs went up the back-stairs and down the front-stairs and had me cornered in the living-room. I managed to get up on to the mantelpiece above the fireplace, but it gave way and came down with a tremendous crash, throwing a large marble clock, several vases, and myself heavily to the floor. Muggs was so alarmed by the racket that when I picked myself up he had disappeared. We couldn't find him anywhere, although we whistled and shouted, until old Mrs. Detweiler called after dinner that night. Muggs had bitten her once, in the leg, and she came into the living-room only after we assured her that Muggs had run away. She had just seated herself when, with a great growling and scratching of claws, Muggs emerged from under a davenport where he had been quietly hiding all the time and bit her again. Mother examined the bite and put arnica on it and told Mrs. Detweiler that it was only a bruise. "He just bumped you," she said. But Mrs. Detweiler left the house in a nasty state of mind.

Lots of people reported our Airedale to the police, but my father held a municipal office at the time and was on friendly terms with the police. Even so, the cops had been out a couple of times—once when Muggs bit Mrs. Rufus Sturtevant and again when he bit Lieutenant-Governor Malloy—but mother told them that it hadn't been Muggs' fault but the fault of the people who were bitten. "When he starts for them, they scream," she explained, "and that excites him." The cops suggested that it might be a good idea to tie the dog up, but mother said that it mortified him to be tied up and that he wouldn't eat when he was tied up.

Muggs at his meals was an unusual sight. Because of the fact that if you reached towards the floor he would bite you, we usually put his plate on top of an old kitchen-table with a bench alongside the table. Muggs would stand on the bench and eat. I remember that my mother's Uncle Horatio, who boasted that he was the third man up Missionary Ridge, was splutteringly indignant when he found out that we fed the dog on a table because we were afraid to put his plate on the floor. He said he wasn't afraid of any dog that ever lived and that he would put the dog's plate on the floor if we would give it to him. Roy said that if Uncle Horatio had fed Muggs on the ground just before the Battle he would have been the first man up Missionary Ridge. Uncle Horatio was furious. "Bring him in! Bring him in now!" he shouted. "I'll feed the —— on the floor!" Roy was all for giving him a chance, but my father wouldn't hear of it. He said that Muggs had already been fed. "I'll feed him again!" bawled Uncle Horatio. We had quite a time quieting him.

In his last year Muggs used to spend practically all of his time outdoors. He didn't like to stay in the house for some reason or other—perhaps it held too many unpleasant memories for him. Anyway, it was hard to get him to come in, and as a result the garbage man, the iceman, and the laundryman wouldn't come near the house. We had to haul the garbage down to the corner, take the laundry out and bring it back, and meet the iceman a block from home. After this had gone on for some time we hit on an ingenious arrangement for getting the dog in the house so that we could lock him up while the gas meter was read, and so on. Muggs was afraid of only one thing, an electrical storm. Thunder and lightning frightened him out of his senses (I think he thought a storm had broken the day the mantelpiece fell). He would rush into the house and hide under the bed or in a clothes closet. So we fixed up a thunder machine out of a long, narrow piece of sheet iron with a wooden handle at one end. Mother would shake this vigorously when she wanted to get Muggs into the house. It made an excellent imitation of thunder, but I suppose it was the most roundabout system for running a household that was ever devised. It took a lot out of mother.

A few months before Muggs died, he got to "seeing things". He would rise slowly from the floor, growling low, and stalk stiff-legged and menacing towards nothing at all. Sometimes the Thing would be just a little to the right or left of a visitor. Once a Fuller Brush salesman got hysterics. Muggs came wandering into the room like Hamlet following his father's ghost. His eyes were fixed on a spot just to the left of the Fuller Brush man, who stood it until Muggs was about three slow, creeping paces from him. Then he shouted. Muggs wavered on past him into the hallway, grumbling to himself, but the Fuller man went on shouting. I think mother had to throw a pan of cold water on him before he stopped. That was the way she used to stop us boys when we got into fights.

Muggs died quite suddenly one night. Mother wanted to bury him in the family lot under a marble stone with some such inscription as "Flights of angels sing thee to thy rest", but we persuaded her it was against the law. In the end we just put up a smooth board above his grave along a lonely road. On the board I wrote with an indelible pencil *Cave Canem*. Mother was quite pleased with the simple classic dignity of the old Latin epitaph.

12 *The Heart of the Shoal*

HERMAN MELVILLE

Now, as many Sperm Whales had been captured off the western coast of Java, in the near vicinity of the Straits of Sunda; indeed, as most of the ground, roundabout, was generally recognized by the fishermen as an excellent spot for cruising; therefore, as the *Pequod* gained more and more upon Java Head, the look-outs were repeatedly hailed, and admonished to keep wide awake. But though the green, palmy cliffs of the land soon loomed on the starboard bow, and with delighted nostrils the fresh cinnamon was snuffed in the air, yet not a single jet was descried. Almost renouncing all thought of falling in with any game hereabouts, the ship had well nigh entered the straits, when the customary cheering cry was heard from aloft, and ere long a spectacle of singular magnificence saluted us.

Broad on both bows, at the distance of some two or three miles, and forming a great semicircle, embracing one half of the level horizon, a continuous chain of whale-jets were up-playing and sparkling in the noon-day air. Unlike the straight perpendicular twin-jets of the Right Whale, which, dividing at top, fall over in two branches, like the cleft drooping boughs of a willow, the single forward-slanting spout of the Sperm Whale presents a thick curled bush of white mist, continually rising and falling away to leeward.

Seen from the *Pequod*'s deck, then, as she would rise on a high hill of the sea, this host of vapoury spouts, individually curling up into the air, and beheld through a blending atmosphere of bluish haze, showed like the thousand cheerful chimneys of some dense metropolis, descried of a balmy autumnal morning, by some horseman on a height.

As marching armies approaching an unfriendly defile in the mountains accelerate their march, all eagerness to place that perilous passage in their rear, and once more expand in comparative security upon the plain; even so did this vast fleet of whales now seem hurrying forward through the straits; gradually contracting the wings of their semicircle, and swimming on, in one solid, but still crescentic centre.

Crowding all sail, the *Pequod* pressed after them; the harpooners handling their weapons, and loudly cheering from the heads of their yet suspended boats. If the wind only held, little doubt had they, that chased through these Straits of Sunda, the vast host would only deploy into the Oriental seas to witness the capture of not a few of their number. And who could tell whether, in that congregated caravan, Moby-Dick himself might not temporarily be swimming, like the worshipped white elephant in the coronation procession of the Siamese! So with stun-sail piled on stun-sail, we sailed along, driving these leviathans before us; when, of a sudden, the voice of Tashtego was heard, loudly directing attention to something in our wake.

Corresponding to the crescent in our van, we beheld another in our rear. It seemed formed of detached white

vapours, rising and falling something like the spouts of
the whales; only they did not so completely come and go;
for they constantly hovered, without finally disappearing.
Levelling his glass at this sight, Ahab quickly revolved in
his pivot-hole, crying, "Aloft there, and rig whips and
buckets to wet the sails; Malays, sir, and after us!"

As if too long lurking behind the headlands, till the
Pequod should fairly have entered the straits, these rascally
Asiatics were now in hot pursuit, to make up for their over-
cautious delay. But when the swift *Pequod*, with a fresh
leading wind, was herself in hot chase; how very kind of
these tawny philanthropists to assist in speeding her on to
her own chosen pursuit—mere riding-whips and rowels
to her, that they were. As with glass under arm, Ahab to-
and-fro paced the deck; in his forward turn beholding the
monsters he chased, and in the after one the bloodthirsty
pirates chasing *him*; some such fancy as the above seemed
his. And when he glanced upon the green walls of the
watery defile in which the ship was then sailing, and be-
thought him that through that gate lay the route to his
vengeance, and beheld, how that through that same gate
he was now both chasing and being chased to his deadly
end; and not only that, but a herd of remorseless wild
pirates and inhuman atheistical devils were infernally
cheering him on with their curses—when all these con-
ceits had passed through his brain, Ahab's brow was left
gaunt and ribbed, like the black sand beach after some
stormy tide has been gnawing it, without being able to
drag the firm thing from its place.

But thoughts like these troubled very few of the reckless
crew; and when, after steadily dropping and dropping the

pirates astern, the *Pequod* at last shot by the vivid green
Cockatoo Point on the Sumatra side, emerging at last
upon the broad waters beyond; then, the harpooners
seemed more to grieve that the swift whales had been
gaining upon the ship, than to rejoice that the ship had so
victoriously gained upon the Malays. But still driving on
in the wake of the whales, at length they seemed abating
their speed; gradually the ship neared them; and the wind
now dying away, word was passed to spring to the boats.
But no sooner did the herd, by some presumed wonderful
instinct of the Sperm Whale, become notified of the three
keels that were after them—though as yet a mile in their
rear—than they rallied again, and forming in close ranks
and battalions, so that their spouts all looked like flashing
lines of stacked bayonets, moved on with redoubled
velocity.

Stripped to our shirts and drawers, we sprang to the
white-ash, and after several hours' pulling were almost
disposed to renounce the chase, when a general pausing
commotion among the whales gave animating tokens that
they were now at last under the influence of that strange
perplexity of inert irresolution, which when the fishermen
perceive it in the whale, they say he is gallied. The com-
pact martial columns in which they had been hitherto
rapidly and steadily swimming were now broken up in
one measureless rout; and like King Porus' elephants in
the Indian battle with Alexander, they seemed going mad
with consternation. In all directions expanding in vast
irregular circles, and aimlessly swimming hither and
thither, by their short, thick spoutings, they plainly be-
trayed their distraction of panic. This was still more

strangely evinced by those of their number who, completely paralysed as it were, helplessly floated like waterlogged dismantled ships on the sea. Had these leviathans been but a flock of simple sheep, pursued over the pasture by three fierce wolves, they could not possibly have evinced such excessive dismay. But this occasional timidity is characteristic of almost all herding creatures. Though banding together in tens of thousands, the lion-maned buffaloes of the West have fled before a solitary horseman. Witness, too, all human beings, how when herded together in the sheepfold of a theatre's pit, they will, at the slightest alarm of fire, rush helter-skelter for the outlets, crowding, trampling, jamming, and remorselessly dashing each other to death. Best, therefore, withhold any amazement at the strangely gallied whales before us, for there is no folly of the beasts of the earth which is not infinitely outdone by the madness of men.

Though many of the whales, as has been said, were in violent motion, yet it is to be observed that as a whole the herd neither advanced nor retreated, but collectively remained in one place. As is customary in those cases, the boats at once separated, each making for some one lone whale on the outskirts of the shoal. In about three minutes' time Queequeg's harpoon was flung; the stricken fish darted blinding spray in our faces, and then running away with us like light, steered straight for the heart of the herd. Though such a movement on the part of the whale struck under such circumstances, is in no wise unprecedented; and indeed is almost always more or less anticipated; yet does it present one of the more perilous vicissitudes of the fishery. For as the swift monster drags you deeper and deeper into the frantic shoal, you bid adieu to circumspect life and only exist in a delirious throb.

As, blind and deaf, the whale plunged forward, as if by sheer power of speed to rid himself of the iron leech that had fastened to him; as we thus tore a white gash in the sea, on all sides menaced as we flew, by the crazed creatures to and fro rushing about us; our beset boat was like a ship mobbed by ice-isles in a tempest, and striving to steer through their complicated channels and straits, knowing not at what moment it may be locked in and crushed.

But not a bit daunted, Queequeg steered us manfully; now sheering off from this monster directly across our route in advance; now edging away from that, whose colossal flukes were suspended over head, while all the time, Starbuck stood up in the bows, lance in hand, pricking out of our way whatever whales he could reach by short darts, for there was no time to make long ones. Nor were the oarsmen quite idle, though their wonted duty was now altogether dispensed with. They chiefly attended to the shouting part of the business. "Out of the way, Commodore!" cried one, to a great dromedary that of a sudden rose bodily to the surface, and for an instant threatened to swamp us. "Hard down with your tail, there!" cried a second to another, which, close to our gunwale, seemed calmly cooling himself with his own fan-like extremity.

All whaleboats carry certain curious contrivances, originally invented by the Nantucket Indians, called druggs. Two thick squares of wood of equal size are stoutly clenched together, so that they cross each other's grain at right angles; a line of considerable length is then

attached to the middle of this block, and the other end of
the line being looped, it can in a moment be fastened to a
harpoon. It is chiefly among gallied whales that this drugg
is used. For then, more whales are close round you than
you can possibly chase at one time. But sperm whales are
not every day encountered; while you may, then, you
must kill all you can. And if you cannot kill them all at
once, you must wing them, so that they can be afterwards
killed at your leisure. Hence it is, that at times like these
the drugg comes into requisition. Our boat was furnished
with three of them. The first and second were successfully
darted, and we saw the whales staggeringly running off,
fettered by the enormous side-long resistance of the towing
drugg. They were cramped like malefactors with the chain
and ball. But upon flinging the third, in the act of tossing
overboard the clumsy wooden block, it caught under one
of the seats of the boat, and in an instant tore it out and
carried it away, dropping the oarsman in the boat's bottom as the seat slid from under him. On both sides the sea
came in at the wounded planks, but we stuffed two or three
drawers and shirts in, and so stopped the leaks for the time.

It had been next to impossible to dart these drugged-
harpoons, were it not that as we advanced into the herd,
our whale's way greatly diminished; moreover, that as
we went still farther and farther from the circumference
of commotion, the direful disorders seemed waning. So
that when at last the jerking harpoon drew out, and the
towing whale sideways vanished; then, with the tapering
force of his parting momentum, we glided between two
whales into the innermost heart of the shoal, as if from
some mountain torrent we had slid into a serene valley

lake. Here the storms in the roaring glens between the outermost whales were heard but not felt. In this central expanse the sea presented that smooth, satin-like surface, called a sleek, produced by the subtle moisture thrown off by the whale in his more quiet moods. Yes, we were now in that enchanted calm which they say lurks at the heart of every commotion. And still in the distracted distance we beheld the tumults of the outer concentric circles, and saw successive pods of whales, eight or ten in each, swiftly going round and round, like multiplied spans of horses in a ring; and so closely shoulder to shoulder, that a Titanic circus-rider might easily have over-arched the middle ones, and so have gone round on their backs. Owing to the density of the crowd of reposing whales, more immediately surrounding the embayed axis of the herd, no possible chance of escape was at present afforded us. We must watch for a breach in the living wall that hemmed us in; the wall that had only admitted us in order to shut us up. Keeping at the centre of the lake, we were occasionally visited by small tame cows and calves; the women and children of this routed host.

Now, inclusive of the occasional wide intervals between the revolving outer circles, and inclusive of the spaces between the various pods in any one of those circles, the entire area at this juncture, embraced by the whole multitude, must have contained at least two or three square miles. At any rate—though indeed such a test at such a time might be deceptive—spoutings might be discovered from our low boat that seemed playing up almost from the rim of the horizon. I mention this circumstance, because, as if the cows and calves had been purposely locked

up in this innermost fold; and as if the wide extent of the
herd had hitherto prevented them from learning the pre-
cise cause of its stopping; or, possibly, being so young,
unsophisticated, and every way innocent and inexperi-
enced; however it may have been, these smaller whales—
now and then visiting our becalmed boat from the margin
of the lake—evinced a wondrous fearlessness and confidence, or else a still becharmed panic which it was impossible not to marvel at. Like household dogs they came
snuffing round us, right up to our gunwales, and touching
them; till it almost seemed that some spell had suddenly
domesticated them. Queequeg patted their foreheads;
Starbuck scratched their backs with his lance; but fearful
of the consequences, for the time refrained from darting it.

But far beneath this wondrous world upon the surface,
another and still stranger world met our eyes as we gazed
over the side. For, suspended in those watery vaults
floated the forms of the nursing mothers of the whales, and
those that by their enormous girth seemed shortly to become mothers. The lake, as I have hinted, was to a considerable depth exceedingly transparent; and as human
infants while suckling will calmly and fixedly gaze away
from the breast, as if leading two different lives at the
time; and while yet drawing mortal nourishment, be still
spiritually feasting upon some unearthly reminiscence;
even so did the young of these whales seem looking up
towards us, but not at us, as if we were but a bit of Gulf-
weed in their new-born sight. Floating on their sides, the
mothers also seemed quietly eyeing us. One of these little
infants, that from certain queer tokens seemed hardly a
day old, might have measured some fourteen feet in length,

and some six feet in girth. He was a little frisky; though as yet his body seemed scarce yet recovered from that irksome position it had so lately occupied in the maternal reticule; where, tail to head, and all ready for the final spring, the unborn whale lies bent like a Tartar's bow. The delicate side-fins, and the palms of his flukes, still freshly retained the plaited crumpled appearance of a baby's ears newly arrived from foreign parts.

13 *Kaa's Hunting*

RUDYARD KIPLING

ALL THAT is told here happened some time before
Mowgli was turned out of the Seeonee wolf-pack,
or revenged himself on Shere Khan the tiger. It
was in the days when Baloo was teaching him the Law of
the Jungle. The big, serious, old brown bear was delighted
to have so quick a pupil, for the young wolves will only
learn as much of the Law of the Jungle as applies to their
own pack and tribe, and run away as soon as they can
repeat the Hunting Verse: "Feet that make no noise;
eyes that can see in the dark; ears that can hear the winds
in their lairs, and sharp white teeth, all these things are

the marks of our brothers except Tabaqui the Jackal and the Hyaena whom we hate." But Mowgli, as a man-cub, had to learn a great deal more than this. Sometimes Bagheera, the Black Panther, would come lounging through the jungle to see how his pet was getting on, and would purr with his head against a tree while Mowgli recited the day's lesson to Baloo. The boy could climb almost as well as he could swim, and swim almost as well as he could run; so Baloo, the Teacher of the Law, taught him the Wood and Water Laws: how to tell a rotten branch from a sound one; how to speak politely to the wild bees when he came upon a hive of them fifty feet above ground; what to say to Mang the Bat when he disturbed him in the branches at midday; and how to warn the water-snakes in the pools before he splashed down among them. None of the Jungle-People like being disturbed, and all are very ready to fly at an intruder. Then, too, Mowgli was taught the Strangers' Hunting Call, which must be repeated aloud till it is answered, whenever one of the Jungle-People hunts outside his own grounds. It means, translated: "Give me leave to hunt here because I am hungry"; and the answer is: "Hunt then for food, but not for pleasure."

All this will show you how much Mowgli had to learn by heart, and he grew very tired of saying the same thing over a hundred times; but, as Baloo said to Bagheera, one day when Mowgli had been cuffed and run off in a temper: "A man-cub is a man-cub, and he must learn *all* the Law of the Jungle."

"But think how small he is," said the Black Panther, who would have spoiled Mowgli if he had had his own way. "How can his little head carry all thy long talk?"

"Is there anything in the jungle too little to be killed? No. That is why I teach him these things, and that is why I hit him, very softly, when he forgets."

"Softly! What does thou know of softness, old Iron-feet?" Bagheera grunted. "His face is all bruised today by thy—softness. Ugh."

"Better he should be bruised from head to foot by me who love him than he should come to harm through ignorance," Baloo answered very earnestly. "I am now teaching him the Master Words of the Jungle that shall protect him with the birds and the Snake-People, and all that hunt on four feet, except his own pack. He can now claim protection, if he will only remember the words, from all in the jungle. Is not that worth a little beating?"

"Well, look to it, then, that thou dost not kill the man-cub. He is no tree-trunk to sharpen thy blunt claws upon. But what are those Master Words? I am more likely to give help than to ask it"—Bagheera stretched out one paw and admired the steel-blue, ripping-chisel talons at the end of it—"still I should like to know."

"I will call Mowgli and he shall say them—if he will. Come, Little Brother!"

"My head is ringing like a bee-tree," said a sullen little voice over their heads, and Mowgli slid down a tree-trunk very angry and indignant, adding as he reached the ground: "I come for Bagheera and not for *thee*, fat old Baloo!"

"That is all one to me," said Baloo, though he was hurt

and grieved. "Tell Bagheera, then, the Master Words of the Jungle that I have taught thee this day."

"Master Words for which people?" said Mowgli, delighted to show off. "The jungle has many tongues. *I* know them all."

"A little thou knowest, but not much. See, O Bagheera, they never thank their teacher. Not one small wolfling has ever come back to thank old Baloo for his teachings. Say the word for the Hunting-People, then—great scholar."

"We be of one blood, ye and I," said Mowgli, giving the words the bear accent which all the hunting-people use.

"Good. Now for the birds."

Mowgli repeated, with the Kite's whistle at the end of the sentence.

"Now for the Snake-People," said Bagheera.

The answer was a perfectly indescribable hiss, and Mowgli kicked up his feet behind, clapped his hands together to applaud himself, and jumped on to Bagheera's back, where he sat sideways, drumming with his heels on the glossy skin and making the worst faces he could think of at Baloo.

"There—there! That was worth a little bruise," said the brown bear tenderly. "Some day thou wilt remember me." Then he turned aside to tell Bagheera how he had begged the Master Words from Hathi the Wild Elephant, who knows all about these things, and how Hathi had taken Mowgli down to a pool to get the Snake Word from a water-snake, because Baloo could not pronounce it, and how Mowgli was now reasonably safe against all accidents in the jungle, because neither snake, bird, nor beast would hurt him.

"No one, then, is to be feared," Baloo wound up, patting his big furry stomach with pride.

"Except his own tribe," said Bagheera, under his breath; and then aloud to Mowgli: "Have a care for my ribs, Little Brother! What is all this dancing up and down?"

Mowgli had been trying to make himself heard by pulling at Bagheera's shoulder-fur and kicking hard. When the two listened to him he was shouting at the top of his voice: "And so I shall have a tribe of my own, and lead them through the branches all day long."

"What is this new folly, little dreamer of dreams?" said Bagheera.

"Yes, and throw branches and dirt at old Baloo," Mowgli went on. "They have promised me this. Ah!"

"*Whoof!*" Baloo's big paw scooped Mowgli off Bagheera's back, and as the boy lay between the big forepaws he could see the Bear was angry.

"Mowgli," said Baloo, "thou hast been talking with the *Bandar-log*—the Monkey People!"

Mowgli looked at Bagheera to see if the Panther was angry too, and Bagheera's eyes were as hard as jade-stones.

"Thou hast been with the Monkey-People—the grey apes—the people without a Law—the eaters of everything. That is a great shame."

"When Baloo hurt my head," said Mowgli (he was still on his back), "I went away, and the grey apes came down from the trees and had pity on me. No one else cared." He snuffled a little.

"The pity of the Monkey-People!" Baloo snorted. "The stillness of the mountain stream! The cool of the summer sun! And then, man cub?"

"And then, and then, they gave me nuts and pleasant things to eat, and they—they carried me in their arms up to the top of the trees and said I was their blood-brother except that I had no tail, and should be their leader some day."

"They have *no* leader," said Bagheera. "They lie. They have always lied."

"They were very kind and they bade me come again. Why have I never been taken among the Monkey-People? They stand on their feet as I do. They do not hit me with hard paws. They play all day. Let me get up! Bad Baloo, let me up! I will play with them again."

"Listen, man cub," said the Bear, and his voice rumbled like thunder on a hot night. "I have taught thee all the Law of the Jungle for all the peoples of the jungle—except the Monkey-Folk who live in the trees. They have no law. They are outcasts. They have no speech of their own, but use the stolen words which they overhear when they listen, and peep, and wait up above in the branches. Their way is not our way. They are without leaders. They have no remembrance. They boast and chatter and pretend that they are a great people about to do great affairs in the jungle, but the falling of a nut turns their minds to laughter and all is forgotten. We of the jungle have no dealings with them. We do not drink where the monkeys drink; we do not go where the monkeys go; we do not hunt where they hunt; we do not die where they die. Hast thou ever heard me speak of the *Bandar-log* till today?"

"No," said Mowgli in a whisper, for the forest was very still now Baloo had finished.

"The Jungle-People put them out of their mouths and out of their minds. They are very many, evil, dirty, shameless, and they desire, if they have any fixed desire, to be noticed by the Jungle-People. But we do *not* notice them even when they throw nuts and filth on our heads."

He had hardly spoken when a shower of nuts and twigs spattered down through the branches.

"The Monkey-People are forbidden," said Baloo, "forbidden to the Jungle-People. Remember."

"Forbidden," said Bagheera, "but I still think Baloo should have warned thee against them."

"I—I? How was I to guess he would play with such dirt? The Monkey-People! Faugh!"

A fresh shower came down on their heads and the two trotted away, taking Mowgli with them. What Baloo had said about the monkeys was perfectly true. They belonged to the tree-tops, and as beasts very seldom look up, there was no occasion for the monkeys and the Jungle-People to cross each other's path. But whenever they found a sick wolf, or a wounded tiger, or bear, the monkeys would torment him, and would throw sticks and nuts at any beast for fun and in the hope of being noticed. Then they would howl and shriek senseless songs, and invite the Jungle-People to climb up their trees and fight them, or would start furious battles over nothing among themselves, and leave the dead monkeys where the Jungle-People could see them. They were always just going to have a leader, and laws and customs of their own, but they never did, because their memories would not hold over from day to day, and so they compromised things by making up a saying: "What the *Bandar-log* think now the jungle will think later," and that comforted them a great deal. None of the beasts would notice, and that was why they were so pleased when Mowgli came to play with them, and they heard how angry Baloo was.

They never meant to do any more—the *Bandar-log* never mean anything at all; but one of them invented what seemed to him a brilliant idea, and he told all the others that Mowgli would be a useful person to keep in the tribe, because he could weave sticks together for protection from the wind; so, if they caught him, they could make him teach them. Of course Mowgli, as a woodcutter's child, inherited all sorts of instincts, and used to make little huts of fallen branches without thinking how he came to do it, and the Monkey-People, watching in the trees, considered his play most wonderful. This time, they said, they were really going to have a leader and become the wisest people in the jungle—so wise that everyone else would notice and envy them. Therefore they followed Baloo and Bagheera and Mowgli through the jungle very quietly till it was time for the midday nap, and Mowgli, who was very much ashamed of himself, slept between the Panther and the Bear, resolving to have no more to do with the Monkey-People.

The next thing he remembered was feeling hands on his legs and arms—hard, strong, little hands—and then a swash of branches in his face, and then he was staring down through the swaying boughs as Baloo woke the jungle with his deep cries and Bagheera bounded up the trunk with every tooth bared. The *Bandar-log* howled with

triumph and scuffled away to the upper branches where
Bagheera dared not follow, shouting: "He has noticed us!
Bagheera has noticed us. All the Jungle-People admire
us for our skill and our cunning." Then they began their
flight; and the flight of the Monkey-People through tree-
land is one of the things nobody can describe. They have
their regular roads and cross-roads, up hills and down
hills, all laid out from fifty to seventy or a hundred feet
above ground, and by these they can travel even at night
if necessary. Two of the strongest monkeys caught Mowgli
under the arms and swung off with him through the tree-
tops, twenty feet at a bound. Had they been alone, they
could have gone twice as fast, but the boy's weight held
them back. Sick and giddy as Mowgli was, he could not
help enjoying the wild rush, though the glimpses of earth
far down below frightened him, and the terrible check and
jerk at the end of the swing over nothing but empty air
brought his heart between his teeth. His escort would
rush him up a tree till he felt the thinnest topmost branches
crackle and bend under them, and then with a cough and
a whoop would fling themselves into the air outward and
downward, and bring up, hanging by their hands or their
feet to the lower limbs of the next tree. Sometimes he
could see for miles and miles across the still green jungle,
as a man on the top of a mast can see for miles across the
sea, and then the branches and leaves would lash him
across the face, and he and his two guards would be almost
down to earth again. So, bounding and crashing and
whooping and yelling, the whole tribe of *Bandar-log* swept
along the tree-roads with Mowgli their prisoner.

For a time he was afraid of being dropped: then he

grew angry but knew better than to struggle, and then he began to think. The first thing was to send back word to Baloo and Bagheera, for, at the pace the monkeys were going, he knew his friends would be left far behind. It was useless to look down, for he could only see the top-sides of the branches, so he stared upward and saw, far away in the blue, Chil the Kite balancing and wheeling as he kept watch over the jungle waiting for things to die. Chil saw that the monkeys were carrying something, and dropped a few hundred yards to find out whether their load was good to eat. He whistled with surprise when he saw Mowgli being dragged up to a tree-top and heard him give the Kite call for—"We be of one blood, thou and I." The waves of the branches closed over the boy, but Chil balanced away to the next tree in time to see the little brown face come up again. "Mark my trail," Mowgli shouted. "Tell Baloo of the Seeonee Pack and Bagheera of the Council Rock."

"In whose name, Brother?" Chil had never seen Mowgli before, though of course he had heard of him.

"Mowgli, the Frog. Man-cub they call me! Mark my tra-il!"

The last words were shrieked as he was being swung through the air, but Chil nodded and rose up till he looked no bigger than a speck of dust, and there he hung, watching with his telescope eyes the swaying of the tree-tops as Mowgli's escort whirled along.

"They never go far," he said with a chuckle. "They never do what they set out to do. Always pecking at new things are the *Bandar-log*. This time, if I have any eyesight, they have pecked down trouble for themselves, for

Baloo is no fledgling and Bagheera can, as I know, kill more than goats."

So he rocked on his wings, his feet gathered up under him, and waited.

Meantime, Baloo and Bagheera were furious with rage and grief. Bagheera climbed as he had never climbed before, but the thin branches broke beneath his weight, and he slipped down, his claws full of bark.

"Why didst thou not warn the man-cub?" he roared to poor Baloo, who had set off at a clumsy trot in the hope of overtaking the monkeys. "What was the use of half slaying him with blows if thou didst not warn him?"

"Haste! O Haste! We—we may catch them yet!" Baloo panted.

"At that speed! It would not tire a wounded cow. Teacher of the Law—cub-beater—a mile of that rolling to and fro would burst thee open. Sit still and think! Make a plan. This is no time for chasing. They may drop him if we follow too close."

"*Arrula! Whoo!* They may have dropped him already, being tired of carrying him. Who can trust the *Bandar-log*? Put dead bats on my head! Give me black bones to eat! Roll me into the hives of the wild bees that I may be stung to death, and bury me with the Hyaena, for I am the most miserable of bears! *Arulala! Wahooa!* O Mowgli, Mowgli, why did I not warn thee against the Monkey-Folk instead of breaking thy head? Now perhaps I may have knocked the day's lesson out of his mind, and he will be alone in the jungle without the Master Words."

Baloo clasped his paws over his ears and rolled to and fro moaning.

"At least he gave me all the Words correctly a little time ago," said Bagheera impatiently. "Baloo, thou hast neither memory nor respect. What would the jungle think if I, the Black Panther, curled myself up like Ikki the Porcupine, and howled?"

"What do I care what the jungle thinks? He may be dead by now."

"Unless and until they drop him from the branches in sport, or kill him out of idleness, I have no fear for the man-cub. He is wise and well-taught, and above all he has the eyes that make the Jungle-People afraid. But (and it is a great evil) he is in the power of the *Bandar-log*, and they, because they live in trees, have no fear of any of our people." Bagheera licked one fore-paw thoughtfully.

"Fool that I am! Oh, fat, brown, root-digging fool that I am," said Baloo, uncurling himself with a jerk, "it is true what Hathi the Wild Elephant says: '*To each his own fear*'; and they, the *Bandar-log*, fear Kaa the Rock Snake. He can climb as well as they can. He steals the young monkeys in the night. The whisper of his name makes their wicked tails cold. Let us go to Kaa."

"What will he do for us? He is not of our tribe, being footless—and with most evil eyes," said Bagheera.

"He is very old and very cunning. Above all, he is always hungry," said Baloo hopefully. "Promise him many goats."

"He sleeps for a month after he has once eaten. He may be asleep now, and even were he awake, what if he would rather kill his own goats?" Bagheera, who did not know much about Kaa, was naturally suspicious.

"Then in that case, thou and I together, old hunter, might make him see reason." Here Baloo rubbed his faded brown shoulder against the Panther, and they went off to look for Kaa the Rock-python.

They found him stretched out on a warm ledge in the afternoon sun, admiring his beautiful new coat, for he had been in retirement for the last ten days, changing his skin, and now he was very splendid—darting his big blunt-nosed head along the ground, and twisting the thirty feet of his body into fantastic knots and curves, and licking his lips as he thought of his dinner to come.

"He has not eaten," said Baloo, with a grunt of relief, as soon as he saw the beautifully mottled brown and yellow jacket. "Be careful, Bagheera! He is always a little blind after he has changed his skin, and very quick to strike."

Kaa was not a poison-snake—in fact, he rather despised the poison-snakes as cowards—but his strength lay in his hug, and when he had once lapped his huge coils round anybody there was no more to be said. "Good hunting!" cried Baloo, sitting up on his haunches. Like all snakes of his breed, Kaa was rather deaf, and did not hear the call at first. Then he curled up ready for any accident, his head lowered.

"Good hunting for us all," he answered. "Oho, Baloo, what dost thou do here? Good hunting, Bagheera. One of us at least needs food. Is there any news of game afoot? A doe now, or even a young buck? I am as empty as a dried well."

"We are hunting," said Baloo carelessly. He knew that you must not hurry Kaa. He is too big.

"Give me permission to come with you," said Kaa. "A

blow more or less is nothing to thee, Bagheera or Baloo, but I—I have to wait and wait for days in a wood-path and climb half a night on the mere chance of a young ape. Pss-haw! The branches are not what they were when I was young. Rotten twigs and dry boughs are they all."

"Maybe thy great weight has something to do with the matter," said Baloo.

"I am a fair length—a fair length," said Kaa, with a little pride. "But for all that it is the fault of this new-grown timber. I came very near to falling on my last hunt—very near indeed—and the noise of my slipping, for my tail was not tight wrapped round the tree, waked the *Bandar-log*, and they called me most evil names."

"Footless, yellow earth-worm," said Bagheera under whiskers, as though he were trying to remember something.

"Sssss! Have they ever called me *that*?" said Kaa.

"Something of that kind it was that they shouted to us last moon, but we never noticed them. They will say anything—even that thou hast lost all thy teeth, and wilt not face anything bigger than a kid, because (they are indeed shameless, these *Bandar-log*)—because thou art afraid of the he-goat's horns," Bagheera went on sweetly.

Now a snake, especially a wary old python like Kaa, very seldom shows that he is angry, but Baloo and Bagheera could see the big swallowing-muscles on either side of Kaa's throat ripple and bulge.

"The *Bandar-log* have shifted their grounds," he said quietly. "When I came up into the sun today I heard them whooping among the treetops."

"It—it is the *Bandar-log* that we follow now," said Baloo; but the words stuck in his throat, for that was the first time in his memory that one of the Jungle-People had owned to being interested in the doings of the monkeys.

"Beyond doubt, then, it is no small thing that takes two such hunters—leaders in their own jungle I am certain—on the trail of the *Bandar-log*," Kaa replied courteously, as he swelled with curiosity.

"Indeed," Baloo began, "I am no more than the old and sometimes very foolish Teacher of the Law to the Seeonee wolf-cubs, and Bagheera here——"

"Is Bagheera," said the Black Panther, and his jaws shut with a snap, for he did not believe in being humble. "The trouble is this, Kaa. Those nut-stealers and pickers of palm leaves have stolen away our man-cub, of whom thou hast perhaps heard."

"I heard some news from Ikki (his quills make him presumptuous) of a man-thing that was entered into a wolf-pack, but I did not believe. Ikki is full of stories half heard and very badly told."

"But it is true. He is such a man-cub as never was," said Baloo. "The best and wisest and boldest of man-cubs—my own pupil, who shall make the name of Baloo famous through all the jungles; and besides, I—we—love him, Kaa."

"Tss! Tss!" said Kaa, shaking his head to and fro. "I also have known what love is. There are tales I could tell that——"

"That need a clear night when we are all well fed to praise properly," said Bagheera quickly. "Our man-cub is in the hands of the *Bandar-log* now, and we know that of all the Jungle-People they fear Kaa alone."

"They fear me alone. They have good reason," said Kaa. "Chattering, foolish, vain—vain, foolish, and chattering, are the monkeys. But a man-thing in their hands is in no good luck. They grow tired of the nuts they pick, and throw them down. They carry a branch half a day, meaning to do great things with it, and then they snap it in two. That man-thing is not to be envied, They called me also—'yellow fish', was it not?"

"Worm—worm—earth-worm," said Bagheera, "as well as other things which I cannot now say for shame."

"We must remind them to speak well of their master. Aaa—sssh! We must help their wandering memories. Now, whither went they with the cub?"

"The jungle alone knows. Towards the sunset, I believe," said Baloo. "We had thought that thou wouldst know, Kaa."

"I? How? I take them when they come in my way, but I do not hunt the *Bandar-log*, or frogs—or green scum on a water-hole for that matter."

"Up, Up! Up, Up! Hillo! Illo! Illo! Illo! Look up, Baloo of the Seeonee Wolf Pack!"

Baloo looked up to see where the voice came from, and there was Chil the Kite, sweeping down with the sun shining on the upturned flanges of his wings. It was near Chil's bed-time, but he had ranged all over the jungle looking for the Bear and had missed him in the thick foliage.

"What is it?" said Baloo.

"I have seen Mowgli among the *Bandar-log*. He bade

me tell you. I watched. The *Bandar-log* have taken him beyond the river to the monkey city—to the Cold Lairs. They may stay there for a night, or ten nights, or an hour. I have told the bats to watch through the dark time. That is my message. Good hunting, all you below!"

"Full gorge and a deep sleep to you, Chil," cried Bagheera. "I will remember thee in my next kill, and put aside the head for thee alone, O best of kites!"

"It is nothing. It is nothing. The boy held the Master Word. I could have done no less," and Chil circled up again to his roost.

"He has not forgotten to use his tongue," said Baloo, with a chuckle of pride. "To think of one so young remembering the Master Word for the birds too while he was being pulled across trees!"

"It was most firmly driven into him," said Bagheera. "But I am proud of him, and now we must go to the Cold Lairs."

They all knew where that place was, but few of the Jungle-People ever went there, because what they called the Cold Lairs was an old deserted city, lost and buried in the jungle, and beasts seldom use a place that men have once used. The wild boar will, but the hunting-tribes do not. Besides, the monkeys lived there as much as they could be said to live anywhere, and no self-respecting animal would come within eye-shot of it except in times of drought, when the half-ruined tanks and reservoirs held a little water.

"It is half a night's journey—at full speed," said Bagheera, and Baloo looked very serious. "I will go as fast as I can," he said anxiously.

"We dare not wait for thee. Follow, Baloo. We must go on the quick-foot—Kaa and I."

"Feet or no feet, I can keep abreast of all thy four," said Kaa shortly. Baloo made one effort to hurry, but had to sit down panting, and so they left him to come on later, while Bagheera hurried forward, at the quick panther-canter. Kaa said nothing, but, strive as Bagheera might, the huge Rock-python held level with him. When they came to a hill-stream, Bagheera gained, because he bounded across while Kaa swam, his head and two feet of his neck clearing the water, but on level ground Kaa made up the distance. .

"By the Broken Lock that freed me," said Bagheera, when twilight had fallen, "thou art no slow goer!"

"I am hungry," said Kaa. "Besides, they called me speckled frog."

"Worm—earth-worm, and yellow to boot."

"All one. Let us go on," and Kaa seemed to pour himself along the ground, finding the shortest road with his steady eyes, and keeping to it.

In the Cold Lairs the Monkey-People were not thinking of Mowgli's friends at all. They had brought the boy to the lost City, and were very pleased with themselves for the time. Mowgli had never seen an Indian city before, and though this was almost a heap of ruins, it seemed very wonderful and splendid. Some king had built it long ago on a little hill. You could still trace the stone causeways that led up to the ruined gates where the last splinters of wood hung to the worn, rusted hinges. Trees had grown into and out of the walls; the battlements were tumbled down and decayed, and wild creepers hung out of the windows of the towers on the walls in bushy hanging clumps.

A great roofless palace crowned the hill, and the marble of the courtyards and the fountains was split, and stained with red and green, and the very cobblestones in the courtyard where the king's elephants used to live had been thrust up and apart by grasses and young trees. From the palace you could see the rows and rows of roofless houses that made up the city looking like empty honeycombs filled with blackness; the shapeless block of stone that had been an idol, in the square where four roads met; the pits and dimples at street-corners where the public wells once stood, and the shattered domes of temples with wild figs sprouting on their sides. The monkeys called the place their city, and pretended to despise the Jungle-People because they lived in the Forest. And yet they never knew what the buildings were made for nor how to use them. They would sit in circles on the hall of the king's council chamber, and scratch for fleas and pretend to be men; or they would run in and out of the roofless houses and collect pieces of plaster and old bricks in a corner, and forget where they had hidden them, and fight and cry in scuffling crowds, and then break off to play up and down the terraces of the king's garden, where they would shake the rose trees and the oranges in sport to see the fruit and flowers fall. They explored all the passages and dark tunnels in the palace and the hundreds of little dark rooms, but they never remembered what they had seen and what they had not; and so drifted about in ones and twos or crowds telling each other that they were doing as men did. They drank at the tanks and made the water all muddy, and then they fought over it, and then they would all rush together in mobs and shout: " There is no one in the jungle so wise and good and clever and strong and gentle as the *Bandar-log.*" Then all would begin again till they grew tired of the city and went back to the tree-tops, hoping the Jungle-People would notice them.

Mowgli, who had been trained under the Law of the Jungle, did not like or understand this kind of life. The monkeys dragged him into the Cold Lairs late in the afternoon, and instead of going to sleep, as Mowgli would have done after a long journey, they joined hands and danced about and sang their foolish songs. One of the monkeys made a speech and told his companions that Mowgli's capture marked a new thing in the history of the *Bandar-log,* for Mowgli was going to show them how to weave sticks and canes together as a protection against rain and cold. Mowgli picked up some creepers and began to work them in and out, and the monkeys tried to imitate; but in a very few minutes they lost interest and began to pull their friends' tails or jump up and down on all fours, coughing.

"I wish to eat," said Mowgli. "I am a stranger in this part of the jungle. Bring me food, or give me leave to hunt here."

Twenty or thirty monkeys bounded away to bring him nuts and wild pawpaws; but they fell to fighting on the road, and it was too much trouble to go back with what was left of the fruit. Mowgli was sore and angry as well as hungry, and he roamed through the empty city giving the Strangers' Hunting Call from time to time, but no one answered him, and Mowgli felt that he had reached a very bad place indeed. "All that Baloo has said about the *Bandar-log* is true," he thought to himself. "They have no Law, no Hunting Call, and no leaders—nothing but foolish words and little picking thievish hands. So if I am starved or killed here, it will be all my own fault. But I must try to return to my own jungle. Baloo will surely beat me, but that is better than chasing silly rose leaves with the *Bandar-log*."

No sooner had he walked to the city wall than the monkeys pulled him back, telling him that he did not know how happy he was, and pinching him to make him grateful. He set his teeth and said nothing, but went with the shouting monkeys to a terrace above the red sandstone reservoirs that were half-full of rain-water. There was a ruined summer-house of white marble in the centre of the terrace, built for queens dead a hundred years ago. The domed roof had half fallen in and blocked up the underground passage from the palace by which the queens used to enter; but the walls were made of screens of marble tracery—beautiful milk-white fretwork, set with agates and cornelians and jasper and lapis lazuli, and as the moon came up behind the hill it shone through the open-work, casting shadows on the ground like black velvet embroidery. Sore, sleepy, and hungry as he was, Mowgli could not help laughing when the *Bandar-log* began, twenty at a time, to tell him how great and wise and strong and gentle they were, and how foolish he was to wish to leave them. "We are great. We are free. We are wonderful. We are the most wonderful people in all the jungle! We all say so, and so it must be true," they shouted. "Now as you are a new listener and can carry our words back to the Jungle-People so that they may notice us in future, we will tell you all about our most excellent selves." Mowgli made no objection, and the monkeys gathered by hundreds and hundreds on the terrace to listen to their own speakers singing the praises of the *Bandar-log*, and whenever a speaker stopped for want of breath they would all shout together: "This is true; we all say so." Mowgli nodded and blinked, and said "Yes" when they asked him a question, and his head spun with the noise. "Tabaqui, the Jackal, must have bitten all these people," he said to himself, "and now they have the madness. Certainly this is *dewanee*, the madness. Do they never go to sleep? Now there is a cloud coming to cover the moon. If it were only a big enough cloud I might try to run away in the darkness. But I am tired."

That same cloud was being watched by two good friends in the ruined ditch below the city wall, for Bagheera and Kaa, knowing well how dangerous the Monkey-People were in large numbers, did not wish to run any risks. The monkeys never fight unless they are a hundred to one, and few in the jungle care for those odds.

"I will go to the west wall," Kaa whispered, "and come down swiftly with the slope of the ground in my favour. They will not throw themselves upon *my* back in their hundreds, but——"

"I know it," said Bagheera. "Would that Baloo were here; but we must do what we can. When that cloud covers the moon I shall go to the terrace. They hold some sort of council there over the boy."

"Good hunting," said Kaa, grimly, and glided away to

the west wall. That happened to be the least ruined of any, and the big snake was delayed awhile before he could find a way up the stones. The cloud hid the moon, and as Mowgli wondered what would come next he heard Bagheera's light feet on the terrace. The Black Panther had raced up the slope almost without a sound and was striking—he knew better than to waste time in biting—right and left among the monkeys, who were seated round Mowgli in circles fifty and sixty deep. There was a howl of fright and rage, and then as Bagheera tripped on the rolling, kicking bodies beneath him, a monkey shouted: "There is only one here! Kill him! Kill." A scuffling mass of monkeys, biting, scratching, tearing, and pulling, closed over Bagheera, while five or six laid hold of Mowgli, dragged him up the wall of the summer-house, and pushed him through the hole of the broken dome. A man-trained boy would have been badly bruised, for the fall was a good fifteen feet, but Mowgli fell as Baloo had taught him to fall, and landed on his feet.

"Stay there," shouted the monkeys, "till we have killed thy friends, and later we will play with thee—if the Poison-People leave thee alive."

"We be of one blood, ye and I," said Mowgli, quickly giving the Snake's Call. He could hear rustling and hissing in the rubbish all round him and gave the Call a second time to make sure.

"Even ssso! Down hoods all!" said half a dozen low voices (every ruin in India becomes sooner or later a dwelling-place of snakes, and the old summer-house was alive with cobras). "Stand still, Little Brother, for thy feet may do us harm."

Mowgli stood as quietly as he could, peering through the open-work and listening to the furious din of the fight round the Black Panther—the yells and chatterings and scufflings, and Bagheera's deep, hoarse cough as he backed and bucked and twisted and plunged under the heaps of his enemies. For the first time since he was born, Bagheera was fighting for his life.

"Baloo must be at hand; Bagheera would not have come alone," Mowgli thought; and then he called aloud: "To the tank, Bagheera. Roll to the water-tanks. Roll and plunge! Get to the water!"

Bagheera heard, and the cry that told him Mowgli was safe gave him new courage. He worked his way desperately, inch by inch, straight for the reservoirs, hitting in silence. Then from the ruined wall nearest the jungle rose up the rumbling war-shout of Baloo. The old Bear had done his best, but he could not come before. "Bagheera," he shouted, "I am here. I climb! I haste! *Ahuwora!* The stones slip under my feet! Wait my coming, O most infamous *Bandar-log!*" He panted up the terrace only to disappear to the head in a wave of monkeys, but he threw himself squarely on his haunches, and, spreading out his fore-paws, hugged as many as he could hold, and then began to hit with a regular *bat-bat-bat*, like the flipping strokes of a paddle-wheel. A crash and a splash told Mowgli that Bagheera had fought his way to the tank where the monkeys could not follow. The Panther lay gasping for breath, his head just out of water, while the monkeys stood three deep on the red steps, dancing up and down with rage, ready to spring upon him from all sides if he came out to help Baloo. It was then that Bagheera lifted up his dripping chin, and in despair gave the Snake's Call for protection—"We be of one blood, ye and I"—for he believed that Kaa had turned tail at the last minute. Even Baloo, half smothered under the monkeys on the edge of the terrace, could not help chuckling as he heard the Black Panther asking for help.

Kaa had only just worked his way over the west wall, landing with a wrench that dislodged a coping-stone into the ditch. He had no intention of losing any advantage of the ground, and coiled and uncoiled himself once or twice, to be sure that every foot of his long body was in working order. All that while the fight with Baloo went on, and the monkeys yelled in the tank round Bagheera, and Mang, the Bat, flying to and fro, carried the news of the great battle over the jungle, till even Hathi the Wild Elephant trumpeted, and far away, scattered bands of the Monkey-Folk woke and came leaping along the tree-roads to help their comrades in the Cold Lairs, and the noise of the fight roused all the day-birds for miles round. Then Kaa came straight, quickly, and anxious to kill. The fighting-strength of a python is in the driving blow of his head backed by all the strength and weight of his body. If you can imagine a lance, or a battering-ram, or a hammer weighing nearly half a ton driven by a cool, quiet mind living in the handle of it, you can roughly imagine what Kaa was like when he fought. A python four or five feet long can knock a man down if he hits him fairly in the chest, and Kaa was thirty feet long, as you know. His first stroke was delivered into the heart of the crowd round Baloo—was sent home with shut mouth in silence, and there was no need of a second. The monkeys scattered with cries of—"Kaa! It is Kaa! Run! Run!"

Generations of monkeys had been scared into good behaviour by the stories their elders told them of Kaa, the night-thief, who could slip along the branches as quietly as moss grows, and steal away the strongest monkey that ever lived; of old Kaa, who could make himself look so like a dead branch or a rotten stump that the wisest were deceived, till the branch caught them. Kaa was everything that the monkeys feared in the jungle, for none of them knew the limits of his power, none of them could look him in the face, and none had ever come alive out of his hug. And so they ran, stammering with terror, to the walls and the roofs of the houses, and Baloo drew a deep breath of relief. His fur was much thicker than Bagheera's, but he had suffered sorely in the fight. Then Kaa opened his mouth for the first time and spoke one long hissing word, and the far-away monkeys, hurrying to the defence of the Cold Lairs, stayed where they were, cowering, till the loaded branches bent and crackled under them. The monkeys on the walls and the empty houses stopped their cries, and in the stillness that fell upon the city Mowgli heard Bagheera shaking his wet sides as he came up from the tank. Then the clamour broke out again. The monkeys leaped higher up the walls; they clung round the necks of the big stone idols and shrieked as they skipped along the battlements, while Mowgli, dancing in the summer-house, put his eye to the screen-work and hooted owl-fashion between his front teeth, to show his derision and contempt.

"Get the man-cub out of that trap; I can do no more," Bagheera gasped. "Let us take the man-cub and go. They may attack again."

"They will not move until I order them. Stay you ssso!" Kaa hissed, and the city was silent once more. "I could not come before, Brother, but I *think* I hear thee call"—this was to Bagheera.

"I—I may have cried out in the battle," Bagheera answered. "Baloo, art thou hurt?"

"I am not sure that they have not pulled me into a hundred little bearlings," said Baloo gravely, shaking one leg after the other. "Wow! I am sore. Kaa, we owe thee, I think, our lives—Bagheera and I."

"No matter. Where is the manling?"

"Here in a trap. I cannot climb out," cried Mowgli. The curve of the broken dome was above his head.

"Take him away. He dances like Mao the Peacock, He will crush our young," said the cobras inside.

"Hah!" said Kaa, with a chuckle, "he has friends everywhere, this manling. Stand back, Manling; and hide you, O Poison People. I break down the wall."

Kaa looked carefully till he found a discoloured crack in the marble tracery showing a weak spot, made two or three light taps with his head to get the distance, and then lifting up six feet of his body clear of the ground, sent home half a dozen full-power, smashing blows, nose-first. The screen-work broke and fell away in a cloud of dust and rubbish, and Mowgli leaped through the opening and flung himself between Baloo and Bagheera—an arm round each big neck.

"Art thou hurt?" said Baloo, hugging him softly.

"I am sore, hungry, and not a little bruised; but, oh they have handled ye grievously, my Brothers! Ye bleed."

"Others also," said Bagheera, licking his lips, and looking at the monkey-dead on the terrace and round the tank.

"It is nothing, it is nothing, if thou art safe, O my pride of all little frogs!" whimpered Baloo.

"Of that we shall judge later," said Bagheera, in a dry voice that Mowgli did not at all like. "But here is Kaa, to whom we owe the battle and thou owest thy life. Thank him according to our customs, Mowgli."

Mowgli turned and saw the great python's head swaying a foot above his own.

"So this is the manling," said Kaa. "Very soft is his skin, and he is not so unlike the *Bandar-log*. Have a care, Manling, that I do not mistake thee for a monkey some twilight when I have newly changed my coat."

"We be of one blood, thou and I," Mowgli answered. "I take my life from thee, tonight. My kill shall be thy kill if ever thou art hungry, O Kaa."

"All thanks, Little Brother," said Kaa, though his eyes twinkled. "And what may so bold a hunter kill? I ask that I may follow when next he goes abroad."

"I kill nothing—I am too little, but I drive goats towards such as can use them. When thou art empty come to me and see if I speak the truth. I have some skill in these (he held out his hands), and if ever thou art in a trap, I may pay the debt which I owe to thee, to Bagheera, and to Baloo, here. Good hunting to ye all, my masters."

"Well said," growled Baloo, for Mowgli had returned thanks very prettily. The python dropped his head lightly for a minute on Mowgli's shoulder. "A brave heart and a courteous tongue," said he. "They shall carry thee far through the jungle, Manling. But now go hence quickly with thy friends. Go and sleep, for the moon sets, and what follows it is not well that thou shouldst see."

The moon was sinking behind the hills, and the lines of trembling monkeys huddled together on the walls and battlements looked like ragged, shaky fringes of things. Baloo went down to the tank for a drink, and Bagheera began to put his fur in order, as Kaa glided out into the centre of the terrace and brought his jaws together with a ringing snap that drew all the monkeys' eyes.

"The moon sets," he said. "Is there yet light to see?"

From the walls came a moan like the wind in the tree-tops: "We see, O Kaa."

"Good. Begins now the Dance—the Dance of the Hunger of Kaa. Sit still and watch."

He turned twice or thrice in a big circle, weaving his head from right to left. Then he began making loops and figures of eight with his body, and soft, oozy triangles that melted into squares and five-sided figures, and coiled mounds, never resting, never hurrying, and never stopping his low, humming song. It grew darker and darker, till at last the dragging, shifting coils disappeared, but they could hear the rustle of the scales.

Baloo and Bagheera stood still as stone, growling in their throats, their neck-hair bristling, and Mowgli watched and wondered

"*Bandar-log*," said the voice of Kaa at last, "can ye stir foot or hand without my order? Speak!"

"Without thy order we cannot stir foot or hand, O Kaa!"

"Good! Come all one pace closer to me."

The lines of the monkeys swayed forward helplessly, and Baloo and Bagheera took one stiff step forward with them.

"Closer!" hissed Kaa, and they all moved again.

Mowgli laid his hands on Baloo and Bagheera to get them away, and the two great beasts started as though they had been waked from a dream.

"Keep thy hand on my shoulder," Bagheera whispered. "Keep it there, or I must go back—must go back to Kaa. Aah!"

"It is only old Kaa making circles on the dust," said Mowgli, "let us go"; and the three slipped off through a gap in the walls to the jungle.

"*Whoof!*" said Baloo, when he stood under the still trees again. "Never more will I make an ally of Kaa," and he shook himself all over.

"He knows more than we," said Bagheera, trembling. "In a little time, had I stayed, I should have walked down his throat."

"Many will walk by that road before the moon rises again," said Baloo. "He will have good hunting—after his own fashion."

"But what was the meaning of it all?" said Mowgli, who did not know anything of a python's powers of fascination. "I saw no more than a big snake making foolish circles till the dark came. And his nose was all sore. Ho! Ho!"

"Mowgli," said Bagheera angrily, "his nose was sore

on *thy* account; as my ears and sides and paws and Baloo's neck and shoulders are bitten on *thy* account. Neither Baloo nor Bagheera will be able to hunt with pleasure for many days."

"It is nothing," said Baloo: "we have the man-cub again."

"True; but he has cost us heavily in time which might have been spent in good hunting, in wounds, in hair—I am half plucked along my back—and last of all, in honour. For, remember, Mowgli, I, who am the Black Panther, was forced to call upon Kaa for protection, and Baloo and I were both made stupid as little birds by the Hunger-Dance. All this, Man-cub, came of thy playing with the *Bandar-log*."

"True; it is true," said Mowgli sorrowfully. "I am an evil man-cub, and my stomach is sad in me."

"*Mf*! What says the Law of the Jungle, Baloo?"

Baloo did not wish to bring Mowgli into any more trouble, but he could not tamper with the Law, so he mumbled: "Sorrow never stays punishment. But remember, Bagheera, he is very little."

"I will remember; but he has done mischief, and blows must be dealt now. Mowgli, hast thou anything to say?"

"Nothing. I did wrong. Baloo and thou are wounded. It is just."

Bagheera gave him half a dozen love-taps; from a panther's point of view they would hardly have waked one of his own cubs, but for a seven-year-old boy they amounted to as severe a beating as you could wish to avoid. When it was all over Mowgli sneezed, and picked himself up without a word.

"Now," said Bagheera, "jump on my back, Little Brother, and we will go home."

One of the beauties of Jungle Law is that punishment settles all scores. There is no nagging afterwards.

Mowgli laid his head down on Bagheera's back and slept so deeply that he never waked when he was put down by Mother Wolf's side in the home-cave.

More Beaver Books

We hope you have enjoyed this Beaver Book. Here are some of the other titles:

A Knight and his Castle What it was like in a castle, by R. Ewart Oakeshott

Travel Quiz A brain-teasing quiz book for all the family on all aspects of travel by plane, train and car

The Twelve Labours of Hercules The adventures of the hero Hercules, beautifully retold by Robert Newman; illustrated superbly by Charles Keeping

Who Knows? Twelve mysteries involving sudden death, mysterious disappearances and hidden treasure, by Jacynth Hope-Simpson

The Call of the Wild The epic story of Buck the great sledge dog in the frozen North, by Jack London

The Last of the Vikings Henry Treece's exciting story, in the saga tradition, about the young Harald Hardrada, King of Norway; with more superb illustrations by Charles Keeping

Ghost Horse Dramatic story about a legendary stallion in the American West, by Joseph E. Chipperfield

New Beavers are published every month and if you would like the *Beaver Bulletin* – which gives all the details – please send a stamped addressed envelope to:

Beaver Bulletin
The Hamlyn Group
Astronaut House
Feltham
Middlesex TW14 9AR

362310